HOW TO STOP SEXUAL HARASSMENT IN OUR SCHOOLS

A Handbook and Curriculum Guide for Administrators and Teachers

Robert J. Shoop
Kansas State University

Debra L. Edwards
Pottawatomi West School District

Allyn and Bacon
Boston • London • Toronto • Sydney • Tokyo • Singapore

ISBN 0-205-15318-6

This publication is designed to provide accurate and authoritative information in regard to the subject matter covered. It is sold with the understanding that neither the author nor the publisher is engaged in rendering legal, accounting, or other professional service. If legal advice or other expert assistance is required, the services of a competent professional person should be sought.

From a Declaration of Principles jointly adopted by a Committee of the American Bar Association and a Committee of Publishers.

Printed in the United States of America

10 9 8 7 6 5 4 3 2 1   98 97 96 95 94

We dedicate this book to the many educators who are working to free our schools from sexual harassment and other forms of discrimination.

Contents

Table of Charts

Acknowledgments

This book is the result of several years of study in the area of sexual harassment in elementary and secondary schools. Although we alone are responsible for the content of this book, we have profited immensely from the research of others and from discussions with family members, friends, colleagues, school teachers and administrators, and elementary and secondary school students.

This book could not have been produced without the help of many people:

Jack Hayhow Jr., our friend, colleague, and collaborator, for his counsel and advice.

Katha Hurt, master teacher, and friend, for reading and making editorial suggestions on the entire manuscript.

David A. Brown for his assistance in developing the concept maps.

Rhonda Thornburrow for her assistance in selecting books to be included in the curriculum.

Ray Short, senior editor at Allyn & Bacon, and Steve Dragin, Associate Publisher at Allyn & Bacon, for their commitment to this book.

We also wish to acknowledge that some of the material in this book is drawn from our earlier writings, especially *Sexual Harassment in Our Schools: What Parents and Teachers Need to Know to Spot it and Stop It*, Shoop and Hayhow (©1993 Allyn & Bacon, Inc.).

Introduction

We wrote this book to help administrators and teachers recognize and respond appropriately to the complex legal and educational issues surrounding sexual harassment in our elementary and secondary schools. Although recent studies have documented that sexual harassment is rampant in our schools, most teachers are not prepared for the minefield of conflicting emotions and attitudes that currently exists regarding appropriate and inappropriate behavior for administrators, teachers and students.

It is clear that behavioral rules are changing in schools. Behavior that was once seen as normal or tolerated as merely rude may now result in educators losing their jobs and or damaging their careers. It is not just new teachers who are unprepared and confused. Many experienced administrators and teachers admit that they don't know what they to should do if they see student-to-student sexual harassment or are victims of harassment themselves.

A growing number of educators are committed to eradicating sexual harassment from their schools. These educators work in school districts that have developed comprehensive school board-approved policies and conducted training sessions for all of their employees, including bus drivers, secretaries, custodians, para-professionals, teachers and administrators. A growing number of school districts know that staff development is only the first step.

These school districts ensure that every student is informed that sexual harassment will not be tolerated and educated about his or her rights and responsibilities in this area. Some of these schools are providing assembly programs and peer education programs. Others are integrating information about sexual harassment into their curricula. These programs focus on assertiveness and career development for female students and offer awareness experiences for male students that focus on peer pressure and the elimination of sexual stereotyping. The training sessions explain what sexual harassment is, why it is prohibited, what students should do if they are harassed, and what the consequences are for students or educators who are guilty of sexual harassment.

Unfortunately, not all school districts take sexual harassment so seriously. Some school boards and superintendents report that they want to "let sleeping dogs lie." Because they have not received any complaints or been sued, they don't see sexual harassment as an important issue. These educators believe that discussing sexual harassment will cause more problems than it will solve.

Others acknowledge that sexual harassment certainly exists in the workplace but do not believe that it occurs in their schools. These people think it happens only in high school, and not in elementary schools. And still others, though competent and concerned educators, do not know what constitutes sexual harassment.

In addition to being concerned that all educators recognize the forms of sexual harassment and the seriousness of the problems they present in our schools, and that they have specific strategies for eradicating it, we are concerned with a new phenomenon. The recent national attention to the problems of sexual harassment has resulted in backlash. Some administrators and teachers report that they are increasingly apprehensive about working closely with colleagues or students of the other gender because they fear that their motives might be misinterpreted. Some male educators tell us they do not want to work with female teachers or students. They especially don't want to work alone with them, travel with them, or attend out-of-town conferences with them because they are afraid of being falsely accused of sexual harassment.

Other administrators and teachers report that they are afraid that angry, street-savvy kids will attempt to blackmail them or intimidate them with threats of sexual harassment charges. Others fear that these threats will be carried out and result in false accusations of sexual harassment. These educators know that even false charges have caused innocent teachers to lose their careers and families. In its most extreme form fear of sexual harassment charges causes teachers to fail to comfort injured children or congratulate successful students. Some school districts have gone so far as to recommend that teachers celebrate a student's progress by shaking hands with no other touching.

At at first glance these fears may seem reasonable, but we believe that in many cases they are examples of what Susan Faludi has identified as an effort to halt or reverse women's quest for equality. Although we admit that there have been and will continue to be false accusations of sexual harassment, we believe that the far more serious issue is the pervasive and destructive power of sexual harassment in our schools.

Sexual harassment is devastating. It can destroy a student's self-concept, an educator's career and a school district's reputation. The consequences of sexual harassment are extreme in the devastation of our daughters. They are extreme in the dysfunctional and counter-productive manner in which our sons are socialized to relate to their mothers, sisters, wives, female friends, and coworkers.

All educators have a professional obligation to know and understand their rights and responsibilities and the rights and responsibilities of their students as they relate to sexual harassment. However, before sexual harassment can be eradicated and prevented, we must understand its causes and consequences.

Although we will briefly address the serious issue of teacher-to-student harassment and the harassment of teachers, this book will focus on eliminating student-to-student sexual harassment. The most compelling reason for this focus is that the majority of sexual harassment in our schools is between students; school-age children are the most vulnerable to harassment. We are confident that sexual harassment at all levels will be reduced if we begin to teach our children appropriate behavior. Educators have a responsibility to protect children while they teach them how to protect themselves.

We focus on schools because people do not suddenly begin harassing as adults. This destructive behavior is learned, and it is learned to a dramatic extent in schools. To eradicate sexual harassment students must learn appropriate behavior very early in life. Our educational system is key to early training. Our schools can and must do more than teach math and science; they must help our children become happy, productive, and cooperative members of society. Each educator and each student then, must allowed to learn in an educational environment that is safe, orderly and free of fear and intimidation.

This book lays out a map of the known territory of sexual harassment in our schools. However, it is a map for an pioneer not a sightseer. It is a map of a territory that has only recently begun to be explored. Our map identifies the major landmarks and sign posts and points out the known pitfalls. It shows some pathways that offer promise for success and warns of the dangers of failing to prepare adequately the journey. We offer a specific plan for implementing a sexual harassment prevention program in your school or school district. We also offer detailed curriculum guides and specific class activities for all grade levels. We ask that educators make a commitment to eradicate sexual harassment from their schools and so expand and improve upon this map.

Part One

**Sexual Harassment: What
Is It and Why Should I Care?**

Chapter One

Sexual Harassment In Our Schools

For years we conducted inservice workshops on various legal issues. Participants frequently stayed after our presentations and asked questions about specific laws or court cases. When we started making presentations in 1988 about educator's rights and responsibilities regarding sexual harassment, we noticed that something quite different was happening. Participants who stayed after the presentations were no longer asking us questions. They were telling us stories. They were telling us about incidents that happened to them or to their children. Some of these stories were about incidents that had taken place fifteen or twenty years ago; some took place that day. Regardless of when the incidents took place they were told with passion and sometimes with tears.

Bill loved to dance. He took jazz and ballet classes from the time he was in the first grade. He was often the only boy in the class but that never bothered him. When his friends put pictures of Montana and Jordan on their walls, Bill put up Nuryev and Baryshinikof posters.

Bill's problems began when he started middle school. Athletics were a very big part of the lives of most of his male friends. Although most were not on a team, they were very big fans of football and basketball. When they heard that Bill was going to be in a dance recital, they started calling him "queer" and "homo." Even some of his teachers made jokes about his interest in dance.

Bill stopped going to his dance classes. He also stopped going to school.

Doug looked up from his science book and announced, "Pussy at 5 o'clock." All five boys sitting at a table in the school library turned to look at Jennifer as she entered the room. As she approached their table they began commenting on her legs, bottom, and breasts.

By the time she was within hearing distance the boys were remarking on her suitability as a sex partner. When Jennifer heard the first comment she stopped in confusion. Her face reddened and she turned and hurried out of the library. As she left the room she heard the boys hooting, whistling and calling after her. The teacher who was supervising the library told the boys to hold down the noise.

Katie and Brad walked hand-in-hand to the kindergarten play area. As the other children began playing on the playground equipment, Brad turned to Katie and said, "Let's play rape. You start to run and I will chase you."

Katie turned and started to run across the playground. Brad gave her a head start then he started running after her yelling "You better run fast! If I catch you, I'm going to rape you."

One of the supervising teachers shook her head in amazement and said, "Brad has been watching too much television."

Cory came home in tears. When her mother asked her what was wrong, Cory just cried harder and ran to her room. Repeated attempts by Cory's mother and father to find out what was wrong were unsuccessful. The next morning Cory said she was sick and could not go to school.

After meeting with Cory's teacher at the middle school and having more talks with Cory, her parents still could not find out what was wrong. Several days later they learned that several boys said Cory "smelled bad" and began calling her "tuna."

Although he was only in the ninth grade, Eric was a natural athlete. The football coach told him his only problem was that he was too small. The coach suggested that if Eric went out for wrestling and lifted weights he would have a good chance of making the football team next year.

Eric went out for the wrestling team and enjoyed the practices. That is, he enjoyed them until Jessica tried out for the team. Jessica was a gifted athlete. Ever since she was six she had been a member of softball, swimming and track teams. Her three older brothers had wrestled in high school and had taught her many wrestling holds.

Eric and Jessica were in the same weight class and had to practice together every night. During the second week of practice, challenge matches were held to determine who would wrestle on the junior varsity team. Jessica pinned Eric in the first period.

By the time Eric got to school the next day everyone knew that a girl had beaten him in wrestling. The teasing became unmerciful. He quit the team, but the teasing did not stop. Eric thought about it for several weeks before he got his father's gun out of the closet and shot himself in the head.

Rhonda was popular with the boys and girls in her sophomore class. On Friday night she went to the home football game with a group of male and female friends. On the way back from the rest room four boys grabbed her and pulled her to the ground. They pulled her sweatshirt and bra up around her neck and wrote their names on her breasts with markers.

Later she told her parents that the thing that bothered her the most was that the boys were her friends and they said they were just having fun.

The boys were suspended from school for two days, and Rhonda was told not to attend any more football games unless she was with her parents.

Teachers and administrators are beginning to see the consequences of sexual harassment and they want to talk about their experiences.

Recently, we began to receive phone calls and letters from school board members, administrators and teachers who had attended our presentations. These educators wanted to know if behaviors that they were observing were examples of sexual harassment. They also asked us what they should do if they were being harassed by their supervisors or colleagues. Some of the most distressing calls came from parents whose children had described incidents of sexual harassment but pleaded with their parents not to do anything because they were embarrassed or were afraid that the situation would become worse. Although it is clear that educators and parents are confused about many issues surrounding sexual harassment, it is equally clear that they are no longer going to remain silent.

If the incidents that were presented at the beginning of this chapter were collected from across the country over a period of several years they would still be heartbreaking. The fact that they all happened in Kansas or Missouri in 1993 make them even more tragic. The heartland of our country, small rural communities, communities where parents and teachers boast of the quality of life and of their outstanding schools, are not immune to the ravages of sexual harassment. What is happening in our society that allows our children to cause each other so much pain? How can children who come from "good homes" act this way? Why don't administrators, teachers, or other students do something to help these victims of sexual harassment?

Extent of the Problem

According to a survey on sexual harassment in schools released in 1993 by the American Association of University Women (AAUW) 85 percent of girls and 76 percent of boys in grades eighth through eleventh have been sexually harassed at school. Although sexual harassment takes a toll on all students, the impact on girls is devastating. According to AAUW Educational Foundation President Alice McKee, "In school a girl doesn't get called on by her teacher, but she is the subject of catcalls; she doesn't hear stories about women of achievement, but she hears rumors about her sexual behavior."

The AAUW report and other recent studies have focused national attention on the long overlooked but very serious problem of sexual harassment in our schools. Behavior that had been unrecognized, ignored or tolerated is now being closely examined. Sexual harassment is now being recognized and understood as a very serious offense. It is not about flirting, humor, raging hormones, or horseplay. It is about power and the harasser's need to exert it over a victim.

Although sexual harassment has always existed, until recently it has had no name. Without a name it was difficult for victims identify the problem and confront their harassers. In 1974 Lin Farley coined the term *sexual harassment* to describe the pattern of unwanted sexual attention by males to females in the workplace. She identified sexual harassment as a violation of the concept of equality --and neutrality in the workplace. In addition, she was the first to address the psychological, sociological, ideological, ethical, legal, and economic consequences of sexual harassment.

Although sexual harassment in the workplace is now widely recognized as a serious issue that must be addressed, the nature and extent of sexual harassment in elementary and secondary schools is only beginning to become known. Sexual harassment in schools is different from sexual harassment in the workplace because: (1) students are required by law to remain in school and (2) because of their age, students are more vulnerable than adults.

According to a fact sheet issued by the AAUW, girls are more frequently and more likely to be sexually harassed in school than are boys, and they are more likely to be harassed in public places. Harassment has an exceedingly negative effect on girls' academic participation and performance and a significant impact on girls' emotions and their feelings about themselves. Girls who have been harassed at school try to avoid having it happen again -- even if it means restricting their choices of where to go or who to be with.

Despite the growing awareness of the problem of sexual harassment, most victims still do not report it. According to the AAUW, students usually do not report sexual harassment to adults. If they tell anyone, most tell a friend. Only seven percent of sexually harassed students told a teacher, and almost one quarter of the victims told no one. Many victims do not report incidents of sexual harassment because they are afraid that they will not be believed. Some are concerned that their friends will ridicule or ostracize them. And others simply do not want to draw attention to themselves. Many victims of sexual harassment do not understand that they have the right to be free from intimidation and hostility.

Many victims would rather try to deal with sexual harassment informally first, but many do not have the necessary skills. In the workplace, victims of sexual harassment are just as likely to change jobs as a result of sexual harassment as they are to take formal action. Students usually do not have the option of leaving school. Consequently, they often suffer in silence.

Today there is a national discussion taking place to determine appropriate and inappropriate behavior in schools. It is no longer acceptable to excuse certain behaviors as the natural activity of adolescent boys, and yet there is a great deal of confusion and controversy around exactly what the new expectations are. Sexual harassment is a complex and hazardous issue. Charges of sexual harassment deal with very sensitive and personal experiences that are often hard to prove. Students, parents, teachers, and administrators are asking their friends, colleagues, and family members: "What exactly is sexual harassment?" "How pervasive is the problem?" "Who are the victims of sexual harassment?" "Who are the harassers?" "What should I do if I am sexually harassed?" "How do I keep from being falsely accused of sexual harassment?"

Although in the majority of sexual harassment cases the victim is a female, the AAUW survey indicates that significant numbers of boys report being targets as well. However, because the vast majority of reported cases involves male harassers and female victims, and because the impact of sexual harassment is greater for girls than boys, we will focus much of our attention on incidents that involve male perpetrators and female victims. Although we often use the male pronoun for the harasser and the female pronoun for the victim, it must be remembered that both sexes can be harassers and victims. It is important to note, too, that same sex sexual harassment is also a serious problem. In fact, much of the sexual harassment of boys is perpetrated by other boys.

Most men don't think of themselves as sexual harassers. Surveys indicate, though, that the majority of men say they have done or said something that a woman might interpret as sexual harassment, even if it was unintentional. Men often react with fear, anger, confusion, exasperation, indignation, or resentment when they are questioned about sexual harassment. Occasionally a male participant at one of our workshops will laugh and say that he would love to be sexually harassed. We usually respond by telling him that with his attitude it would be impossible for him to be sexually harassed because the behavior must be unwelcome. If he persists in his claim we have responded by telling him that we can arrange for him to be sexually harassed, but he will not know when or where it will happen nor will he know who he will be with or what he will be doing. We make it clear that he will have absolutely no control over who the harasser is or what type of harassment he will receive. So far we have not had any volunteers.

It is not our intention to place blame for sexual harassment. We know that most educators oppose discrimination and believe in fairness. We also believe that most educators will join in efforts to eradicate sexual harassment because it is the right thing to do.

It is critically important that every school district have a formal plan for eradicating sexual harassment. This plan must include a written policy prohibiting all forms of sexual harassment. The policy must clearly identify unacceptable behavior and be widely distributed throughout the school district. All school employees and students must know that sexual harassment is prohibited and that there will be serious consequences if it occurs. School districts must also have educational programs on sexual harassment for their students, parents, faculty, and staff. We must prepare our daughters and sons to know their rights and empower them to stand up for these rights. We must educate our sons and daughters to respect themselves and their fellow students.

Legal Interpretation of Sexual Harassment

Sexual harassment is any unwelcome behavior of a sexual nature that interferes with your life. The term "unwelcome" indicates the action or behavior was unsolicited and nonreciprocal. In other words, the person witnessing or being affected by the behavior didn't "ask for" or invite the behavior, nor did the person respond "in kind" with similar behavior. For example, wanted kissing, touching, or flirting, is not sexual harassment.

"Behavior of a sexual nature" includes virtually any conduct that refers to sex. Such conduct can include using profane language or telling off-color jokes. It includes using sexist terms such as "babe" or "bitch," or "bimbo" or making comments about body parts. But, it can also include what some may consider to be "terms of endearment" such as "honey," "baby," "darling," etc. Behavior of a sexual nature includes leering and ogling, and without question, any kind of unwanted touching such as patting, hugging, and pinching. Finally, any request for sexual favors in return for benefits meets the criteria established for sexual harassment.

Courts have held that sexual harassment is discriminatory behavior that violates Title VII of the Equal Rights Act of 1964, Title IX of the Education Amendments of 1972, the Fourteenth Amendment to the U. S. Constitution, and various state and local human rights acts. Title VII prohibits discrimination in employment. Even though Congress passed the act in 1964, it was not until 1979 that Catharine MacKinnon, a law professor and a pioneer in the development of sexual harassment legal theory, conceived of sexual harassment as a form of sexual discrimination. Although the concept of sexual harassment is not completely settled in law or fully understood by society as a whole, courts have clearly and consistently affirmed that the workplace and the school must be free from sexual harassment.

Title IX was enacted to combat the widespread discrimination against women in all aspects of education. It protects students in educational settings from sexual harassment in essentially the same manner as Title VII protects employees in the workplace. In the 1992 landmark case of *Franklin v. Gwinnett Public School District*, the Supreme Court ruled that schools can be held liable for monetary and compensatory damages resulting from a teacher's sexual harassment of a student. While the facts of the case spoke exclusively to teacher-to-student harassment, the *Gwinnett* decision has generally been interpreted to hold that schools are liable for all types of harassment, including student-to-student, teacher-to-teacher, and student-to-teacher. The 14th Amendment of the U.S. Constitution provides for equal protection for all people. This amendment essentially says that a person's rights cannot be taken without due process of law.

While not legally required to do so, the courts tend to look to the Equal Employment Opportunity Commission (EEOC) for guidance on matters relating to sexual harassment. In 1988 the EEOC issued a document to all field offices entitled *Policy Guidance on Current Issues of Sexual Harassment..* The document outlined the behavior that constitutes sexual harassment. The guidelines reminded field personnel that sexual harassment is a form or subset of sexual discrimination and is therefore prohibited by Title VII of the 1964 Civil Rights Act. The guidelines went on to say that:

> *Unwelcome sexual advances, requests for sexual favors and other verbal or physical contact of a sexual nature constitute sexual harassment when (1) submission to such conduct is made either explicitly or implicitly a term or condition of an individual's employment, (2)*

submission or rejection of such conduct by an individual is used as the basis for employment decisions affecting such individual, or (3) such conduct has the purpose or effect of unreasonably interfering with an individual's work performance or creating an intimidating, hostile, or offensive working environment.

The EEOC drew upon a substantial body of judicial reasoning in holding that Title VII affords the right to work in an environment free from discriminatory intimidation, ridicule, and insult. The student's workplace is school, and consequently students are afforded this same right.

Three distinct forms of sexual harassment have evolved from the EEOC guidelines and from recent court decisions. Often these forms overlap or occur simultaneously. However, each is a distinct category and provides for a separate complaint or cause of action. The following is a brief introduction to each category of sexual harassment.

* ***Quid Pro Quo*** - *Quid pro quo* is a Latin term often used in law. It means, essentially, "you do something for me and I'll do something for you." In the context of sexual harassment of students, *quid pro quo* may include an offer of special treatment such as awarding a better grade in return for sexual favors. It can also be a threat of retaliation. For example, *quid pro quo* occurs if a teacher threatens to lower a grade or refuses to write a letter of recommendation because a student rejects a sexual request. *Quid pro quo* also takes place if a teacher threatens a student with some penalty if she does not consent to have a sexual relationship with him. One critical aspect of *quid pro quo* is that a single event constitutes a violation. If a teacher makes a sexual proposition that involves the student's educational conditions even one time, *quid pro quo* sexual harassment has occurred. In *quid pro quo* sexual harassment the deprivation of educational benefits, once such deprivation is proven, allows the victim to ask the court to provide relief.

It should be noted that the discussion of *quid pro quo* in schools broaches the subject of teachers having sex with students. It raises questions regarding rape, sexual abuse, sex with a minor, and other equally serious issues. These topics involve areas of law other than sexual harassment and will not be discussed in this book. While most discussions about sexual harassment remind us that in order to be considered sexual harassment the sexual attention must be unwanted, in the school context welcomeness becomes a more important consideration, because most students are minors. Teachers and students should be prevented from any sexual contact on the basis of the professional obligation that teachers have to act in the place of the parent while the child is in the care of the school. In addition to interfering with the teaching process and violating the trust that is necessary in a teacher-student relationship, it is ethically abhorrent.

Hostile Educational Environment - Hostile educational environment is the most prevalent and misunderstood form of sexual harassment. For practical purposes, any sexually-oriented conduct or any sexually-oriented atmosphere that is intimidating or offensive to a reasonable woman, can be construed as creating a hostile educational environment. This concept is confusing because men and women often perceive the very same behavior in quite different ways. What a man might consider innocuous, a woman might consider blatantly offensive. It is important to remember that courts now tend to favor the victim's point of view.

The opinion of a "reasonably prudent woman" is considered in the court's decisions. One critical dimension of the hostile educational environment category is that sexual harassment can occur even though the victim does not suffer any loss of economic or tangible benefits. Unlike *quid pro quo*, hostile educational environment requires a consistent pattern of behavior. A single event does not necessarily constitute a violation. In order for a behavior to be considered to have created a hostile educational environment, it must be "sufficiently pervasive and severe."

* Sexual Favoritism - Although many authors categorize sexual harassment as either *quid pro quo* or hostile educational environment, we believe it is helpful to identify a third category, sexual favoritism. Sexual favoritism is a manifestation of a hostile educational environment but it has some important distinctions and can therefore be viewed as a separate category. Sexual favoritism occurs when a student receives preferential opportunities or benefits as a result of submission to a teacher's sexual advances. In these circumstances, a student who is having a consensual relationship with a teacher or who is voluntarily engaging in flirting behavior may be given special treatment in the form of higher grades or other benefits. Given this situation, it is the other students who are not receiving the same preferential treatment as the student involved in the relationship that are the victims of sexual harassment.

Reasonable Woman Test

In later chapters we will spend more time discussing the standard that courts use to determine if sexual harassment has occurred. However, at this point a few words need to be said about the difference between the reasonable man and the reasonable woman test. In cases of negligence the courts have historically asked, "What would a reasonable man (sometimes modified to 'reasonable person') do in a similar situation?" For example, if a person walking down the sidewalk in front of your home was injured as a result of falling into an unmarked hole that was created by your effort to plant a tree, a court would likely rule that you are liable for the injury to the walker. This decision is based on the belief that a "reasonable person" in a similar situation would have been able to foresee the likelihood that the hole presented a danger. This reasonable person would then have taken steps to warn pedestrians of the hole and thus prevent the injury.

In early sexual harassment cases many courts examined behaviors offensive to women in light of this test. As we mentioned earlier and will discuss later, men and women often see the same situation quite differently. Therefore, because many men did not see anything wrong with the allegedly offensive behavior, courts often ruled that the behavior did not violate the "reasonable man" standard, and therefore no harassment took place.

Recently courts have begun to hold that the appropriate standard in sexual harassment is "Would a reasonable person of the same sex as the victim (in most cases a woman) find the behavior unreasonable?" When we present training sessions on this aspect of sexual harassment, men often say, "If I didn't mean anything offensive, how can it be sexual harassment?" Men also express resentment and confusion when they say, "How are we to know what to do? One woman may thank me for a compliment, and another may get angry and charge me with sexual harassment." One way to gain some understanding about this dilemma is to look at the concept of comfort zone.

Comfort Zones ✓

Since courts are beginning to define sexual harassment from the perspective of the person who is being harassed, a few things must be said about how women perceive sexual harassment. Not all women perceive all of the same behaviors as sexual harassment. A study conducted by Beth Schneider revealed that over 92 percent of the women surveyed viewed sexual assault, sexual propositions, and pinching or grabbing as sexual harassment. However, only 64 percent viewed being stared at or looked over as sexual harassment, and only 53 percent saw joking about a person's body or appearance as sexual harassment. This study indicates that there is some ambivalence and little consensus among women on what constitutes sexual harassment in their day-to-day interactions. Slightly less than 50 percent viewed touching or hugging as sexual harassment and only one in four women considered requests for dates to be sexual harassment.

All people have a series of comfort zones that they draw around themselves. Normally, we allow people to get closer to us and interact more personally only as we feel more comfortable with them. In a casual conversation with a stranger we are likely to share little personal information, allow no touching, and keep a fair amount of space between ourselves and the stranger. As we feel more comfortable with a person and get to know them better, we are likely to allow them to stand closer to us, perhaps put a hand on our shoulder and even joke or tease us. It is only our dearest friends or family members that are given permission to enter the closest circle of intimacy.

We accept the behaviors of others and reciprocate those behaviors only if they fall within the comfort zone that we have developed to deal with that individual. Each of us have different comfort zones. We each select who will enter our comfort zone and for what purpose. Problems can arise when we think that because we have included someone in our comfort zone, they have an obligation to include us in theirs. For example, a female student may indicate that she is upset because a male acquaintance, seeing her in distress, put his arms around her and gave her a hug. Clearly, in this situation the boy meant no harm; in fact, he was offering kindness. However, the girl responded by pulling away, or may even have accused the boy of sexual harassment. Another male student may make the same gesture and the same girl will appreciate his thoughtfulness and return the hug. She has a friendship that allows her to feel safe with the second boy and is therefore willing to allow him further into her comfort zone.

In another situation, a close male friend might tell a female student, "You look really nice in that sweater," and she might feel complimented. She has allowed him inside of her comfort zone by giving him permission to comment on her physical appearance. However, another male student may make a similar comment and the same girl may put it outside the comfort zone and be offended.

According to Gordon W. Allport, "Few people keep their antipathies entirely to themselves." Prejudice will somehow, somewhere find expression in action. These actions have distinguishable degrees that range from passivity to extreme violence. We have used Allport's stages of prejudice as a way of describing how milder forms of sexual harassment, if left uncorrected, may develop into more serious forms.

Allport's stages of prejudice and our parallel stages of sexual harassment follow:

(1) **Antilocution** - talking negatively about a group. We doubt that much can be done to intervene in the private conversations of men about women. However, it is in these conversations that the seeds of sexual harassment are planted. Locker room humor, sexist jokes, and ribald stories lay the foundation for men to consciously and subconsciously think of women only in sexual terms, and more specifically, in terms of derision and ridicule.

(2) **Avoidance** - making conscious efforts to avoid members of the disliked group. Historically we have taught boys that there are boy activities and girl activities. Many boys are still conditioned to stay away from activities that are stereotyped as feminine (i.e. dance, music, art, poetry, etc.) Because they are discouraged from such interaction with females, boys have little first-hand experience with girls as equals.

(3) **Discrimination** - undertaking to exclude all members of the group in question from certain types of employment or other social privileges. Courts have made significant progress in eliminating "male only" social and professional groups. This is very helpful because, by keeping women out, these groups reinforced the separateness between men and women. It is easier to discriminate against an outsider group than it is an insider group.

(4) **Physical attack** - attacking personally or using other forms of violence or semiviolence. Sexual harassment is a form of attack. Whether it is verbal or physical, it harms people. It is our belief that most boys and men would not sexually harass women if they had a better understanding of how their behavior hurts women.

Physical assault and rape are the most extreme form of physical attack.

(5) **Extermination** - displaying the ultimate expression of prejudice. We are not comfortable making the leap to this last stage of prejudice. However, it is obvious that some sexual violence ends in the murder of the victim.

Although Allport did not claim that his five-point scale is mathematically constructed, he used it to call attention to the enormous range of activities that may result from prejudice. Although many people may never move from antilocution to avoidance, or from avoidance to a higher level on the scale, *activity on one level makes the transition to a more intense level easier.*

Sexual harassment often emanates from these contentious relations. In this context, sexual harassment may be used as a way for men to express hostility or anger. Men may also harass to demonstrate their power or to compensate for their lack of power. This form of harassment can be particularly destructive because it is often directed at a victim who was not involved in the original conflict. The victim of the harassment is, many times, a woman in a subordinate position to the harasser and generally a person with limited resources to defend herself. So we see that conflicts between men and women have the potential to provoke widespread harassment.

We also find that what we call cultural conflict causes trouble in relationships between men and women. These cultural conflicts relate more to the structure of our society than to any personal enmity. Underlying these cultural conflicts are preconceptions about "the way things should be." For example, some men still cling to the belief that women should be "barefoot and pregnant." If a man holding such a belief finds himself in competition with a woman for a promotion, he may respond with inordinate hostility. Even though the hostility is caused by the societal structure that allows women to compete with men, the competing woman will bear the brunt of the hostility. Often this hostility takes the form of sexual harassment.

Chapter Two

Causes of Sexual Harassment

In the past, most educators didn't think much about sexual harassment. There were, of course, rude boys and teachers with "Roman hands," but even in the most obvious circumstances, these objectionable actions were generally viewed as personal problems rather than institutional problems. Because there was no term to describe the offensive behavior, it was difficult for women and girls to confront their harassers. Behavior that is now recognized as sexual harassment was often treated as an unavoidable fact of life in our schools and on our playgrounds. A colleague reports:

> "I rode the school bus everyday from kindergarten through my senior year of high school. When I was in second and third grade, a junior high boy constantly teased me. He would sit next to me or in the seat directly behind me and make jokes about my appearance which escalated into shoving and pushing.
>
> I ignored the behavior because the only adult that I told, my mother, said that the boy would stop when he got bored and saw that it wasn't bothering me. Well he never got bored, and it always bothered me."

Until very recently, when students complained about being harassed by their fellow students, they were told to ignore the behavior or to avoid the offending students. When the harasser was a teacher, the behavior was too often labeled a minor character flaw and forgiven.

Today much of society recognizes that students should not have to endure hostile conditions at school. Behavior that was formerly attributed almost exclusively to individual misconduct has been correctly classified as a school problem. For example, the 1993 AAUW report on sexual harassment in our schools conveys that sexual harassment is an experience common to the vast majority of high school students. The most alarming finding of the survey is that fully four out of five students report that they have been the target of some form of sexual harassment during their school lives. Of those students who reported experiencing harassment, "one in four report being targeted 'often.' " According to this survey, "A student's first experience with sexual harassment is most likely to occur in the middle school/junior high years....(however,) some students first experienced unwanted advances before the third grade."

What Causes Sexual Harassment

We believe that sexual harassment is more about power than it is about sex. To a very large extent, students adopt the attitudes accepted by and expressed within their culture. The narcotic of peer pressure is incredibly strong. Students who come to school and observe sexual harassment as a routine behavior of their peers will likely adopt similar behaviors. This is especially true if they have been raised in an atmosphere of male dominance and female subservience. Children raised in homes where women are treated as "second class citizens" bring these attitudes and behaviors to school with them. And if teachers reinforce these attitudes they will become even more ingrained.

The outmoded idea that females are naturally dependent on males may have come from the image of the savage cave man dragging a cave woman by the hair. Whether or not this image has any basis in historical fact, it is the image that best symbolizes the view of the aggressive man and passive woman. While the species and the civilization have evolved considerably in a few thousand years, powerful vestiges of male dominance are alive and well. The deeply ingrained idea of man as the powerful protector of woman has been a compelling and pervasive component of every child's education and socialization. Too often the hidden curriculum of our schools teaches our students that power over women is a basic right and responsibility of manhood.

One of the most blatant examples of the perpetuation of male dominance and female subservience is seen in Helen Andelin's book *Fascinating Womanhood.* This book was written for the instruction of young women. As you read the following quotes keep in mind that they are from a 1992 edition of the book.

> *"Feminine dependency is the feminine actions of a woman. It can best be described by saying, 'It is her lack of masculine ability.' The role of man, we have learned, is to lead, protect and provide for woman. Her need for his manly care is called feminine dependency.*
> *Don't think that protecting a dependent woman is an imposition on a man.* **This most pleasant sensation a real man can experience is his consciousness of this power to give his manly care and protection. Rob him of this sensation of superior strength and ability and you rob him of his manliness.** *(original emphasis) It is a delight to him to protect and shelter a dependent woman. The bigger, manlier and more sensible a man is, the more he seems to be attracted by this quality."*

The back cover of this book announces that, "*Fascinating Womanhood* offers guidance for a new generation of women, happy, fulfilled, adored, and cherished, who want to rediscover the magic of their own feminine selves." With more than two million copies in print, we can't help but wonder how many hundreds of thousands of boys and girls are being influenced by these ideas. The above paragraphs are representative of the message presented in this book. In addition to telling young women that men want to protect dependent women, Andelin tells women how men feel in the presence of capable women.

> "*What happens when the average red-blooded man comes in contact with an obviously able, intellectual and competent woman manifestly independent of any help a mere man can give and capable of meeting him or defeating him upon his own ground? He simply doesn't feel like a man any longer. In the presence of such strength and ability in a mere woman, he feels like a futile, ineffectual imitation of a man. It is the most uncomfortable and humiliating sensation a man can experience; so that the woman who arouses it becomes repugnant to him.*"

We could take some comfort if we could discard the above comments as isolated remarks by someone from an ancient civilization. However our society, whether we intend or not, still teaches our sons that lack of power over women makes them less of a man. We teach our children that boys get to make the rules and girls must obey them. The many methods, subtle and blatant, conscious and unconscious, by which this occurs are discussed later in this book. However, a recent conversation we had with a colleague serves to illustrate the point:

> "*My daughter has always been a leader. She has been a member of the student council and was the*

president of the council at her middle school. At first she was pleased when she was elected to the student council in high school. However, after attending several parties where some of the boys laughed at her and told her 'girls may think they can rule the world, but they can't,' she decided that she was not interested in continuing in student council next year."

Adult male teachers and young males on the playground face a painful paradox. Their very definition of manhood involves power over women, and yet they find themselves answering to female bosses or being told that a girl is going to be the captain of their team.

When a man or boy whose self-concept revolves around power over women is faced with a drastically different reality, they often feel threatened. They may see their choices limited either to battling the perceived threat with whatever weapons they have available or retreating from the threatening environment.

Men and boys make both choices every day. In our schools, boys pressure girls to stay out of certain classes and activities. When girls do gain admission to formerly all-male activities, boys often drop out.

Running from the threatening environment may require substantial effort and time, but the fight response can be initiated at once. Often this fight response takes the form of sexual harassment or other forms of sexual violence.

If parents and teachers continue to perpetuate the paradigm of male dominance and female subservience, if young women are conditioned to accept the idea that power over women is integral to the masculine role, and if men continue to perceive female authority as a threat, sexual harassment will continue to permeate our schools and our society.

Sexual Stereotyping

We are confident that the vast majority of educators believe that all people, are worthy of equal dignity, opportunity, and respect. However, it must be recognized that all people are not the same. We agree with Stephen Bergman and Janet Surrey when they state that before stereotypes can be broken we must "acknowledge differences in experience, perceptions, and power. Denial interferes with dialogue, engagement, and real understanding. It is critical to distinguish stereotype from difference."

Although some of our differences are individual, others are gender-related. According to psychologist David McClelland, "Sex-role turns out to be one of the most important determinants of behavior; psychologists have found sex differences in their studies from the moment they started doing empirical research." In many cases, gender-related differences are the core ingredient of female-male conflict. For that reason, awareness of these gender-related differences becomes critically important.

The fact that men and women experience the world differently may be partially explained by the fact that women and men are trying to accomplish widely varied goals. Deborah Tannen believes that many men tend to see the world as a hierarchial social order where they are either "one up or one down." According to Tannen's theory, the objective of conversation for men is to gain the upper hand and resist attempts from others to push them around. For men, life is very much a struggle to preserve independence and avoid failure. On the other hand, according to Tannen, many women see the same conversation as an opportunity to initiate or strengthen a connection. For many women conversation is a way to achieve closeness. Talking provides the opportunity to seek and give confirmation and support. For many women, life is community. The struggle within the sphere of the community is to preserve intimacy and avoid isolation.

Tannen suggests these differences can be understood in a framework of status or connection. Men are continually attempting to achieve and maintain status; women are continually attempting to establish and maintain connection, to include themselves as a part of an interdependent group. Men, in attempting to achieve status, take aggressive action to demonstrate how they are different (better) than others. Women, because of their desire to be a part of the group, minimize differences and promote egalitarian attitudes. To men, independence is foremost; to women, intimacy is foremost. Given these widely divergent ideas and objectives, it's easy to see how there is often disagreement about what is right and how one should act.

These differences between men and women can be seen early in life. At a very young age, boys and girls tend to play in different ways. Boys tend to play in large groups, often outside, with one boy leading and the rest following. The hierarchy is established and maintained by the boy who can give the orders and make others follow. Boys play games with rules, games that almost always have winners and losers. And, in an effort to attain status, even in the early years, boys will often boast and argue about their skill.

Girls, on the other hand, play in small groups or in pairs. They often negotiate the rules which are generally subordinated to the feelings of each individual. Most of the games have no winners or losers. Girls often just sit together and talk; they seldom boast or challenge each other directly. The differences in girls' and boys' play was well stated by Jean Piaget when he suggested that boys' games are more concerned with rules while girls' games are more concerned with relationships. The differences most of us have observed in the play activities of boys and girls have also been documented by Janet Lever. According to her "these differences are readily apparent and seemingly ingrained by the time children are ten years old." But the differences may, in fact, emerge much earlier than that. According to the studies of Robert Stoller, gender identity, that unchanging core of personality development, is "with rare exception firmly and irreversibly established for both sexes by the time a child is around three years old."

Carol Gilligan's research suggests that these nearly universal differences between the sexes can be explained by the fact that women are primarily responsible for early child care. From the first moments of life, girls have the feeling that "I'm like you, we're connected." Gilligan, suggests that "...girls, in identifying themselves as female, experience themselves as like their mothers, thus fusing the experience of *attachment* with the process of identity formation ...." The concept of being a woman is inextricably woven into the experience of being connected to other people. What is right and what a person should do rest on a foundation of attachment.

The experience for male children is quite different. From the first moments of a little boy's life, he has the experience of "I'm different from you; we're separate." As a result, according to Nancy Chodorow, male development involves a "more emphatic individualization and a more defensive firming of experienced ego boundaries." The concept of being a man is firmly rooted in achieving and maintaining separation. What is right and what a person should do rests on a foundation of independence.

These divergent views about what is right provide the impetus for misunderstanding and controversy. There is, however, another gender-related difference that may contribute even more to cross-gender belligerence. It reveals itself in what Gilligan describes as moral choice. Through the observation of moral choice, we can glimpse the difference in how men and women perceive the world, how they make choices based on those perceptions, and how they behave as a result of the choices.

According to Gilligan, men and women tend to make moral choices using different criteria. She suggests that women tend to embrace a care perspective while men tend to employ a justice perspective. She believes that female decisions are based primarily on the resulting effect of those decisions on other people. The fundamental questions in a care perspective would appear to be...How does this decision make other people feel? What impact will this action have on other people? Gilligan concludes that "...women not only define themselves in a context of human relationship, but also judge themselves in terms of their ability to care."

Men, on the other hand, seek answers to moral choices using a context of rights and rules. If the rules dictate a certain decision, the feelings of the people involved have little relevance. Central to a justice perspective are the questions... "Does this decision conform with the established rules?" "Is this fair?" Clearly, these distinctly different decision-making criteria, can and do lead to different conclusions and actions and may result in hostility.

Differences between men and women can set the stage for conflict. We have observed this same behavior in classes that are traditionally male dominated, and which are taught by males. We were observing a furniture construction class that had two female students and fourteen male students. Each time one of the female students asked the teacher for help, the male teacher would not make suggestions, offer advice, or give encouragement. He would, instead, step in front of the student and proceed to fix the problem. We can't be sure if this behavior was based on the teacher's belief that the female students were genetically incompetent and it would thus be a "waste of time" to teach them, or, if the teacher's need to be in control outweighed his responsibility to teach. In the same class we observed that when male students asked for help, the teacher offered only minimal physical assistance. The teacher sent the clear message that the boys could "figure it out" for themselves.

Finally, we have discovered that what men perceive as threatening is quite different from what women perceive as threatening. Referring once again to Gilligan's work, we find that men and women may perceive danger in different social situations. Men are more likely to be threatened by situations of intimacy or personal affiliation while women may feel threatened by isolation. Male responses to a threat of intimacy might take the form of rudeness, overt hostility, sexual harassment, or even physical attack. While we certainly cannot predict an exact response when intimacy threatens a man's primary goal of independence, we should not be surprised by retaliatory behavior.

Sexual Harassment Map

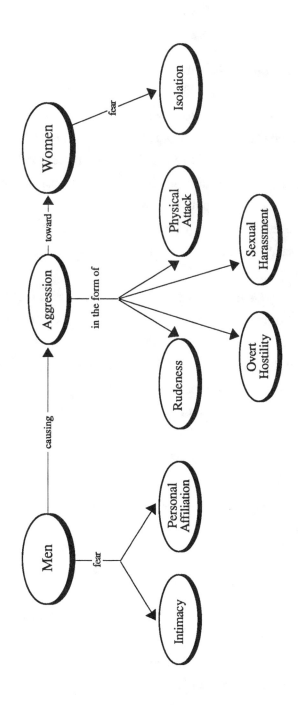

Sex Role Stereotyping

Social scientists borrowed the term *role* from the French theater, where it referred to the roll of paper that contained the actor's part. Today we see a role as the pattern of behavior that a person is expected, encouraged, or trained to perform. According to Deborah David and Robert Brannon, roles involve very few exact behaviors. They are usually general, but clear, guidelines regulating how a person should behave. Just as actors consciously learn the role that is written by the playwright, children learn their roles by observing adults. They also learn from others who are playing complementary roles.

David and Brannon believe that learning how to "play the role of male or female" is the most complex, and demanding role that children must learn. Children start learning their roles at birth and spend a good part of their lives perfecting the assigned sex-roles. The costumes, props, and rewards are quite different for boys and girls. From the time a newborn baby girl is wrapped in a pink blanket and her brother in a blue blanket, the two children are treated differently. Baby girls are often treated as if they are much more fragile than baby boys. Many times toddler boys are told, "Big boys don't cry," while toddler girls are cuddled at the first whimper or sign of a tear. While these incidents may not by themselves produce ill effects, they are indicative of a pattern of differing expectations for each sex. We all recognize how quickly children learn what is expected of them.

Where there is some tolerance for "mistakes" in how boys and girls learn their roles as young children, there is much less tolerance during adolescence. Teenagers can be incredibly cruel to their peers who don't dress, walk, speak, look, eat, or relax in the "acceptable" way. Sex-roles and sex-role stereotypes are forged and tempered in the crucible of middle school and high school.

This realization increases in importance when we recognize that to a large extent sex-role stereotyping is so deeply woven into the fabric of our society that many of us are not even aware of it. In fact, most people think of these roles as innate and genetic rather than learned. Sex role learning is the only explanation for such behaviors as boys holding doors open and girls wearing make-up. This unconscious learning begins to harden into unexamined behaviors and expectations for the behaviors of others. Boys learn that the masculine role includes the fact that they belong to the superior sex. Strong-willed girls challenge sex-role stereotyping at the risk of having their spirits broken. After studying societies all over the world anthropologist Margaret Mead concluded that:

> *"Many, if not all, of the personality traits which we have called masculine or feminine are as lightly linked to sex as are the clothing, the manners, and the form of head-dress that a society at a given period assigns to either sex...the evidence is overwhelmingly in the favor of social conditioning."*

Children interpret the world and their place in the world from their surroundings. They learn how to conduct themselves by watching the people in their lives. If parents and teachers expect boys to play baseball and girls to play with dolls, that is what the children are likely to do.

Now there is absolutely nothing wrong with boys playing baseball and girls playing with dolls. However, if boys are taught it is unmanly to play with dolls, and girls are taught it is unfeminine to play baseball, the children will begin to define themselves by what they do rather than by who they are. If, when these children go to school, their parents and teachers expect boys, but not girls, to be interested in math, we have a serious and far-reaching problem. The critical point is that our common, socially acceptable expectations tend to limit what boys and girls can accomplish. Our expectations, what we can very correctly identify as sex-role stereotyping, can and do rob children of opportunity. While this is true for both sexes, it is more true for girls. Society seems to embrace a lot more "girls can't, or shouldn't" ideas than "boys can't or shouldn't" ideas. For example, society often communicates the message that, "girls don't do very well in science." This message is sent so often and in so many ways that fully capable girls tend to stay away from science courses and later denies them, as women, the opportunity to participate in science-related professions. Most parents and educators are not consciously trying to deny opportunity to female children; they, too, are products of the conditioning of their own parents and teachers.

Sexism

A father and his son were in a car accident. The father was killed and the son seriously injured. The father was pronounced dead at the scene of the accident and his body taken to a local mortuary. The son was taken by ambulance to a hospital and was immediately wheeled into the operating room. A surgeon was called. Upon seeing the patient, the surgeon exclaimed, "Oh my God, it's my son!"

Because many of us process information on the basis of sex-roles, we may have been momentarily confused by the above story. We may have failed to associate the concept of surgeon with the concept of woman.

This momentary confusion is an example of how sexism is often a subconscious ideology, a set of beliefs that we accept implicitly, without question. We're usually unaware of the acceptance of such beliefs because we can't conceive alternatives. Sexism is a prejudice based on a faulty and inflexible generalization about members of one sex. A sexist person is one who uses sex as a criterion to make evaluations and normative judgements about another person.

Sexism has the effect of placing women in an inferior position. The prejudice and stereotyping inherent in sexism (coupled with a culture that embraces the concept of male dominance) causes many men to view women as less than their male counterparts. This perception of women as inferior seems to provide some men with the belief that they have license to abuse and denigrate women through attitude, language, and physical conduct. Such treatment can range from excluding women from work groups to sexual harassment to rape.

Sexism is one of the most significant factors in the perpetuation of sexual harassment. If we are really interested in protecting our children; if we really believe that all people are worthy of equal opportunity, dignity, and respect; and if we are really interested in a better way to live; then we must come to understand the devastating role sexism plays in our lives.

An Early Lesson In Sexual Stereotyping

Allison's pigtails bounced up and down as she ran to the car, opened the door, hopped up and slid onto the front seat. I enjoyed picking her up from school and taking her to her sitter. Mary and I, like most parents, were anxious for her first year of school to go well. We believed that a good first experience with school would go a long way toward ensuring future successes. We were both nervous about sharing teaching responsibilities with someone we didn't know. We had many questions:

*Will her teacher be competent? Will she like Allison?
Will Allison do well in school? Will she like school?*

*As she fastened her seat belt, I asked her how her
day went.*

*"Great, I like school! Mrs. Lamb let me help her
collect the lunch money today!"*

*"Do you know any of the other kids in your
room?"*

*"Oh, yes! Kristin's desk is right next to mine,
and Andrea and Ben and another kid from T-Ball are in
my class, too."*

"What else did you like about school today?"

"Well, we played dog again."

*"Dog? I don't think I know that game. How do
you play it?"*

*"It's lots of fun. The girls that are playing stand
next to one of the boys. Then a boy throws a stick
across the playground, and the girls race each other to
fetch it. The girl who gets to the stick first brings it back
to the boy."*

*Perhaps I was jumping to conclusions. I took a
deep breath and said, "Oh. That's an interesting game.
Do the girls ever get to throw the stick?"*

*"No, just the boys. It's fun. I like to run
around."*

*I caught my breath and could feel myself
becoming anxious. We had raised Allison to believe that
boys and girls are equal. We had taught her that she can
become whatever she wants to be. We tried to use only
nonsexist language and to help her understand the
consequences of sexism. Equity was not just talk in our
house. Allison had helped stuff envelopes for women
political candidates and had marched in NOW
demonstrations. Now, after one week of kindergarten,
she is fetching sticks thrown by boys!*

*During the rest of my day that conversation kept
running through my head. I could not stop thinking
about how many lessons that are taught and learned in
school are not in the curriculum guides. I became more
and more concerned as I thought about how each lesson
learned creates the foundation for future lessons.*

There is another aspect of sexism and sex-role stereotyping
that can be very damaging. It has to do with the messages we

communicate in schools about the proper role and importance of women in our society. As one example, let's consider the seemingly harmless activity of an all-girl cheer leading squad. Of course there are a number of very positive elements involved with cheerleading. However, we also need to be aware of other not so positive messages inherent in this activity. In many ways cheerleading communicates that the proper role for girls is to cheer the boys on to victory. The central concept of female cheerleaders for male sports is that boys are responsible for achievement and girls are responsible for supporting the boys. This idea is reinforced if it is traditional for the female cheerleaders to decorate the male athlete's lockers and send them letters of support.

It is very positive to have activities that encourage students to support one another. However, if the issue is support, why don't we have all-boy cheerleading squads leading the cheers for the girls' basketball team? Just as in the story about Allison and the game called Dog, some school activities create the perception that girls should be subordinate to boys. The social structure in many schools strongly suggests that girls should support boys as the boys strive to achieve.

This message can be subtle, or as is true in the following example, this message can be blatant. During a discussion about sexual harassment in schools, a high school teacher related this story.

> *"I teach in a school where the athletic program has a fund raising event every year. The female students are expected to participate in a 'slave day.' During this day, boys bring dog collars and leashes to school and lead the girls around as the girls carry the boys' books and do their other bidding. Many of the girls wear signs that say, 'So-and-so is my master."*

Think this is a pretty clear example of the way schools teach girls that they are somehow less competent than boys, but we wanted to know what girls thought of this practice. We conducted a survey of two hundred high school girls at a midwest high school, and asked them to read a scenario describing slave day. We then asked the girls to rate the degree to which they were offended on a scale from 1 (inoffensive) to 10 (very offensive.) The average rating for this scenario was 7.7. When asked how they would feel if this activity went on in their school, 31 percent said they would be angry, 26 percent said they would be annoyed, and 10 percent said they would be degraded.

Schools often send the message that females are not as important as males. According to the AAUW report *How Schools Shortchange Girls*, textbooks undervalue and under-represent material on women. When women do appear, their lives are often trivialized and distorted. If students are constantly barraged with the message that women's lives count for less than men's lives, the results can be devastating. If girls believe themselves capable of less; they will attempt less. If girls are instructed that people like themselves (other women and girls) are less important and not worth studying, we can understand how they adopt a diminished self-concept. Low self-esteem is particularly destructive because a strong self-concept is the very core of achievement.

While girls are learning that they are not as valuable as boys, boys are learning that they are more important than girls and come to believe that girls don't have the same rights. This distorted perception results boys adopting harassing behaviors.

Harassing behavior serves to identify men as a member of the ruling group to whom the streets and the school hallways belong. Like other forms of sexual violence, sexual harassment is more about power than it is about sex. The astonishing behavior of moaning, jumping, whistling, singing, winking, contorting face and body, hissing obscenities, laughing hysterically and mumbling hoarse endearments to perfect strangers with no apparent provocation are examples of this pattern of intimidation.

Behavioral Perceptions

Women and men often interpret the same behavior differently. Men and boys tend to perceive interactions that occur in social, business, and academic settings in more sexual terms than do women. According to Catherine Johnson, Margaret Stockdale, and Frank Saal, "When women attempt to create a friendly atmosphere at work or school, that behavior may be interpreted as sexual interest or availability. Men may then act on these misperceptions in a way that is offensive to women and that women label as sexual harassment." According to Frank Saal, Catherine Johnson, and Nancy Weber, "As a woman's behavior becomes more friendly and outgoing when she acclimates to her work or academic environment, men may be quicker to label her behavior as 'sexy' and then to respond in ways the woman construes to be sexually harassing." Other research indicates that men are more likely than women to ascribe responsibility for a sexual harassment incident to the female victim.

In addition to interpreting the same behavior differently, men and women also have different views on the appropriate responses to offensive conduct. Susan Fisk discusses these differences in terms of category-based responses in the human thought and perceptual process. When a man categorizes a female based on her sex, they are evaluating her in terms of characteristics that comport with stereotypes assigned to women rather than in terms of her individual skills or performance. Therefore, if a man categorizes a female along the lines of stereotyped sex-roles, he produces an evaluation of her suitability as a "woman" who might be expected to be sexy, affectionate, and attractive. Females are evaluated less favorably if they do not conform to preconceived stereotypes, regardless of their job performance. According to Margaret Mead, men treat a woman who has power as someone who has to be cajoled, and a woman without power as someone who can be coerced. Unfortunately, our experience with public schools leads us to believe that Mead's observations are still accurate today.

As early as 1978 Mead attributed the problem of sexual harassment to the socialization process of boys and girls. She believed that parents and teachers were teaching boys to respond to women in inappropriate ways. An example indicating that this attitude persists today can be seen in the following comments made to the authors by the mother of a six-year-old girl.

> *"My daughter's birthday is right on the cut-off for getting into kindergarten. When I took her to school to ask the teachers and principal for their suggestions regarding enrolling her or holding her out, the male principal said, in front of my daughter, 'I would hold her out. She is pretty small and if you enroll her now her breasts will not be as developed as her classmates when she begins to go to junior high school'."*

Differences in Perception

Some apparent differences in perception are the result of sexual stereotyping. According to Fiske, there are four preconditions that enhance the presence of stereotyping. These categories are (1) rarity, (2) priming, (3) environment structure, and (4) ambience of the environment.

Rarity exists when an individual's group is smaller in number than its contrasting group so that each individual member is seen as one of a kind. A female student taking a course that has traditionally been identified as a "male course" illustrates the concept of rarity. Because the female student is a clear minority, she is more likely to be harassed by her fellow students and teachers.

Priming means that the educational environment contains objects that encourage stereotypical thinking. Such objects would include photographs of nude and partially nude women, sexual joking, and sexual slurs. If the school environment is contaminated in this way, males will be more likely to view female students as sex objects and interact with them accordingly.

The third precondition for an increased frequency of stereotyping is the nature of the power structure or hierarchy in the school environment. If teachers and administrators tolerate or engage in harassing behavior, students will feel free to sexually harass their fellow students.

And, finally, tolerance of inappropriate conduct promotes the stereotyping of women as sex-objects. The likelihood of stereotyping increases if complaints about sexual harassment are trivialized. We recently received a phone call from the mother of a high school student. She told us the following story:

> *"My daughter, Linda, is in high school. During one of her classes the teacher said, 'Today we are going to talk about the difference between wants and needs. For example, Linda may want me, but she might not need me. Which is it, Linda, do you want me or do you need me?' Many of the students, particularly the boys, laughed.*

Linda came home was very upset and told me what happened. I went to the school's principal and told him how upset Linda, her father, and I were about what we thought was inappropriate behavior.

At first the principal said, 'Oh, that's just that teacher's sense of humor. You shouldn't get so upset because 'I'm sure that the teacher did not mean anything by his comments.' When I made it clear that I did not care what the teacher's intentions were, the principal agreed to speak to the teacher.

The next day the teacher began the class by saying, 'Class, I've been told that I must apologize to Linda. It appears that she and her mother don't have much of a sense of humor. I guess we are not going to be able to joke around in here anymore because of Linda.'"

This incident clearly demonstrates how the educational climate of the school allows sexism and sexual harassment to flourish. If no significant action is taken as a result of female student complaints about graffiti, language, or photos, the harassing behavior will continue and intensify.

How We Interpret Each Other

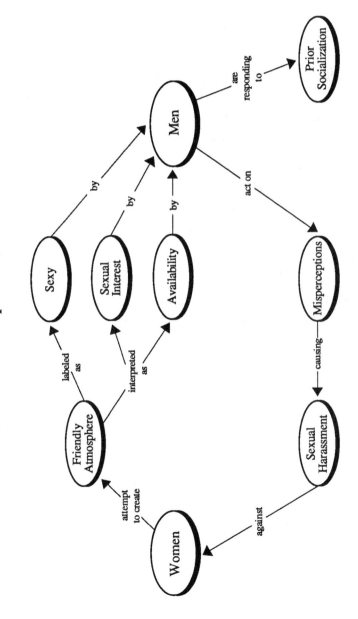

Characteristics of a Sexual Harasser

Although we run the risk of stereotyping by making generalizations about sexual harassers, there have been several studies that have identified common elements among them. In a survey conducted in *Seventeen* magazine, Nan Stein, Nancy Marshall, and Linda Tropp found that only four percent of the reported incidents of sexual harassment in schools were committed by teachers, counselors, or administrators. Most harassment was committed by fellow students.

According to the AAUW report, *Hostile Hallways*, only 18 percent of students who reported being sexually harassed say that they were harassed by a school employee such as a teacher, coach, bus driver, teacher's aide, security guard, principal, or counselor. "Of those who say they have been harassed, nearly four in five have been targeted by a current or former student at school. Among girls who have been harassed: 81 percent report having been harassed by a male acting alone, 57 percent by a group of males, 11 percent by a mixed group of males and females, 10 percent by a female acting alone, and three percent by a group of females." It is interesting to note that the AAUW survey found that of the students who admit to having harassed a fellow student, 94 percent claim that they themselves had been harassed.

More harassment occurs in environments where there are high percentages of men. This is consistent with our experience that female students are more likely to be harassed in classes or programs that have been traditionally dominated by males.

Chapter Three

Consequences of Sexual Harassment

Extent of the Problem

It is not difficult to find examples of sexual harassment in schools. A shocking, although not unusual, account was reported by Tania Silva in a 1992 article that appeared in the *Gainesville Sun.*

> *"At a school board meeting, a 14-year-old student reported that she could no longer wear a skirt to school. 'The boys pull it up over my hips while others laugh. Now when I wear pants, they back me into a corner and pull them down and start to feel me all over....I'm scared, ashamed, and I feel humiliated.'"*

Ralph Hess reports that sexual harassment in schools ranges from teasing to torment. Boys back girls against walls and make gestures between the girls' legs simulating intercourse, reach under shirts to grab breasts, and force girls to pass through lined-up groups of harassers. Recently, a father told us this story:

> *"My daughter came home Friday night and told us what happened to her at school. She said a group of her eighth-grade classmates started chasing her around the room in first hour. They were trying to pull her pants down. She kept running away and trying to get to her seat so that she could sit down. This happened*

before each class. Finally, before the start of fourth hour they succeeded in pulling her pants and underwear down around her knees. She became so angry that she chased them and hit them with her fists. This took place in the classroom while the teacher was out in the hall. When the teacher came in, she stopped the hitting, found out what happened, and took the boys to the office. When my daughter finished the story she started to cry. She doesn't want to go back to school."

Victims of sexual harassment change their attitudes about school, their classmates, and themselves. Imagine what it must be like to know that you will be threatened, ridiculed, or degraded by your peers. Being the victim of sexual harassment results in a sense of helplessness and lowered self-esteem. According to the National School Safety Center, "In an attempt to escape the harassment, the victim plans activities around an avoidance schedule. Her inability to stop the harassment results in anger, humiliation, and shame. A sense of betrayal and stigmatization often result in isolation and withdrawal from others. Those few who stand up and fight often lose the battle, thereby reinforcing the feelings of helplessness generated by the abuse."

At a recent workshop which we conducted for a group of teachers and social workers, a male participant commented, "Sexual harassment is really not such a big deal. After all, it's all in fun and no harm is intended." We asked him if he had a daughter. He said he did and began to tell us about how well she was doing in school. We interrupted him and asked if he could bring her to the next session so we could get a look at her tits.

Educators talk about the "teachable moment" as that point in time when the learner is fully ready to grasp the concept. We have never seen a more dramatic "teachable moment." The man's face got red and he looked as if he were going to come out of his chair and throw a punch. Then he simply said, "Oh, I get it!" We apologized to him for our offensive remark. We then used our remark and his response to begin a discussion about why many men seem to have a difficult time understanding the seriousness of sexual harassment. As long as men see sexual harassment as something that happens to people that they don't know, it is less likely that they will actually "get it."

Many men seem to divide their lives into a variety of watertight compartments. This idea of compartmentalized life can help explain how the above mentioned man could dismiss the sexual harassment of strangers as trivial while becoming highly agitated at the thought of his daughter being sexually harassed.

Sexual harassment is occurring virtually every moment of every day in almost every elementary and secondary school in America. Girls are touched, commented upon, and propositioned. Boys comment on breasts and vaginas and make sexual requests. Some people still believe that girls secretly like this type of attention. Others think that if girls don't like it, they most certainly provoke it with their clothing, their manner of walking, or their behavior. Until recently harassment was recognized as rude, offensive, and impolite, but it was not illegal. However, the rules have changed and sexual harassment in elementary and secondary schools is now against the law.

Occurrence of Sexual Harassment

Recent research indicates that sexual harassment has reached epidemic proportions in our classrooms. It goes on all the time in school - not just teachers harassing students but students harassing students. Sexual harassment is a daily occurrence on school buses and in hallways, in classrooms and laboratories, in gyms and on playing fields. The number of sexual harassment complaints is skyrocketing with a commensurate increase in the number and amount of monetary awards given to compensate victims.

Most sexual harassment in our schools goes unreported. Why would this be so? Why do female students endure the trauma of sexual harassment? Many do not understand what is happening to them. They know that they are made to feel badly. They know that they are being treated differently just because they are girls. But in most cases the school has done nothing to make them believe that their complaints will be taken seriously. Girls often feel that reporting sexual harassment will cause them more embarrassment than enduring the harassment. Many believe that reporting incidents of sexual harassment may result in their being criticized rather than helped with the problem. Young females want to be accepted by males and other females, and if they complain, they assume boys will look upon them as uncooperative, as someone who can't get along. The psychological aspect of sexual harassment is strong. Young women may come to doubt themselves, question the way they handled the situation, or think that they brought the harassment on themselves.

Sexual harassment wreaks havoc on a number of fronts and in a number of different ways. Perhaps the most obvious debilitating manifestation is the physical and emotional harm perpetrated on the victim. Another result of sexual harassment is the denial of equal opportunity to its victims. Our daughters simply do not have the same educational opportunity as do our sons. Time and time again, sexism and sexual harassment deprive girls of their legal right to an equal education.

Sexual harassment also deprives girls of the opportunity for a fair and equitable education. This occurs in a number of different ways. Sometimes girls simply can't face the torture any longer, and they leave school completely. In these cases, sexual harassment deprives the victim of not only an equal education, but of any education at all. Often, however, girls who are harassed attempt to escape the harassment by abandoning certain classes or fields of study. The following report is an extreme example of the consequences of sexual harassment of a female in a non-traditional class.

> *Kelly is a student in the auto body repair class. Her teacher told her to move a 100 lb. box of parts. She wanted to prove that she could do it. She knew that all the boys were watching her. After several failed attempts she gave one more try. She ripped open her intestines and was rushed to the hospital. After surgery and an extensive recovery period she learned that none of the boys would have lifted the box.*

Sexual harassment can be a significant deterrent to students who enroll in non-traditional programs. Is it fair that students should be so intimidated that they feel compelled to leave a class? How can educational opportunity ever be equal for boys and girls when certain classes are off limits? The answer, of course, is that as long as sexual harassment exists in our schools, equal educational opportunity will never be achieved.

There are additional, more subtle ways in which sexual harassment and other forms of sexual discrimination deny equal education. Most of these stem from sex-role stereotyping and other sexist notions so prevalent in our society. For example, teachers routinely give more attention to boys than to girls in the classroom setting. In January of 1993, *Twins* magazine reported on research conducted by Myra and David Sadker. Their research revealed startling evidence of classroom gender bias. According to Myra Sadker, "Teachers give boys more attention than girls. Boys get more constructive help and are asked more probing questions to help them get the answers. Praise for appearance was the only area we found girls got more attention. We also found that boys got more criticism, which when handled well can be very helpful to children." When researchers asked why boys got more criticism teachers said they were afraid girls would cry. The unfortunate upshot is that girls never get a chance to learn how to handle criticism. Other research indicates that teachers treat boys more seriously and validate their thoughts more frequently.

These and other destructive influences have the effect of discouraging girls from pursuing certain endeavors and limiting their achievement when they do. While elementary school girls consistently score equal to boys in standardized testing for math, by the time the students reach middle school, boys have forged ahead. We have no evidence to suggest that the disparity in achievement comes from anything other than gender bias, in the classroom and in society.

> *"I've been sexually harassed for almost three years. One guy kept going around the school telling everyone that I gave him head. It made me feel really embarrassed and sad. I didn't know what to do, so I didn't do anything."*
>
> *14 year old*

> *"My art teacher is constantly telling sick jokes, hugging female students, patting or pinching their butts, looking down their shirts, lifting up skirts, and telling female students how pretty they*

are. It makes me feel degraded and angry. I told my friends about it, but no one else."

15 year old

"This one guy kept asking me out, making obscene comments and finally would kiss his fingers and wipe them on my mouth. I talked to my friends and finally told the teacher. The boy was moved to a seat farther away from me, but nothing else happened to him."

17 year old

"I asked a teacher to help me with my assignment. He said he couldn't, because he's married. I was bewildered at first and when I realized what he was saying and how he was looking at me I was mad. I dropped out of his class and have not taken any other classes from him."

16 year old

The above comments were written in the spring of 1993 in response to a questionnaire we distributed in several mid-west high schools. Even the most callous person can recognize the pain and trauma in these words. These examples of sexual harassment are preventing these students from receiving all of the educational benefits they deserve. It must be remembered that when we talk about sexual harassment in schools, we're talking about real kids and real harm. We're talking about young people whose physical and emotional health is in grave jeopardy. And we are talking about students who feel helpless and hopeless.

According to the AAUW survey, 64 percent of the female victims of sexual harassment report suffering embarrassment. Similarly, 52 percent report that sexual harassment has caused them to feel self-conscious, and 43 percent of the girls report that sexual harassment makes them feel less sure or less confident about themselves. The above findings, alone, should certainly motivate us to work to eliminate sexual harassment from our schools. The report goes on to reveal findings that should motivate us to act more quickly and with the undeniable knowledge that sexual harassment is having grave consequences on its victims.

Of the girls participating in the survey, 39 percent report that sexual harassment has caused them to feel afraid or scared, and 30 percent say that sexual harassment has caused them to doubt whether they can have a happy romantic relationship. As we said earlier, boys are also the victims of sexual harassment, but the AAUW study documents that the consequences of harassment are not nearly as serious for boys as they are for girls. For example, while 39 percent of the girls reported feeling afraid or scared, only eight percent of the boys expressed their feelings this way. When students were asked how they felt right after being harassed, 70 percent of the girls reported being "very upset" or "somewhat upset," compared with only 24 percent of boys.

When a person is constantly attacked and has no effective defense, certain predictable results can occur. As you might expect, the victim often develops a sense of fear and hopelessness. This hopelessness carries potentially grave consequences. Tamara Coder-Mikinski reports on a study that indicates children with a high sense of hopelessness are at greater risk for suicide, depression, and overall psychopathology. A victim of sexual harassment often feels incompetent to deal with the abusive situation. This feeling of incompetence is often transferred to other life areas. A good student may begin to doubt her ability to deal with the challenges of her education, so her grades fall. She may be unwilling to take the normal risks associated with developing healthy relationships so she becomes isolated from her friends. When the victims' pleas for help are ignored, and she receives no support in her effort to stop the harassment, she may begin to feel that she is unworthy of help, that she deserves the treatment she receives.

These feelings of incompetence and lack of worth are the classic descriptions of low self-esteem. Boys and girls have equal self-esteem between the ages of 7 and 11, but that soon changes. According to *How Schools Shortchange Girls*, "by early adolescence, girl's self-esteem has fallen significantly compared to that of boys." The socialization process (including sex-role stereotyping and sexual harassment) has robbed young women of the positive self-image and healthy self-concept so critical to growth, development, and achievement.

Physical and Psychological Costs

Each person has a subjective perception about themselves that influences how they evaluate their own behavior. It is natural for people to judge themselves in terms of their own worthiness or unworthiness. Self-esteem is the term used to describe the degree to which a people admire, or respect, or like themselves.

People who have high self-esteem view themselves as important, valuable, and worthy of respect. Although they recognize their limitations, they believe they will succeed anyway. On the other hand, people with low self-esteem view themselves as unimportant, unlikable, and unworthy of respect. These people don't think that they can control very much in their lives, and, consequently, do not think they can achieve success in reaching their goals. Self-esteem is a very strong motivator. There is a consensus among sociologists that self-esteem is the strongest and most important of all sentiments and drives. Kaplan reflects this consensus when he refers to self-esteem as "...universally and characteristically a dominant motive in the individual's motivational system."

To a large extent a person's self-concept is developed during the time that he or she is going to school. According to Coopersmith, in order for children to develop high self-esteem they must receive unconditional acceptance by significant others which is demonstrated by warmth, encouragement, attention, and affection. They must also have the flexibility and freedom to explore within clearly established and enforced limits and rules. High expectations with respect to academic performance, and parental self-esteem are also very important in developing a strong self-concept.

Children are significantly influenced by the attitudes and feedback of significant others, and over the course of time they come to view themselves as they are viewed by others. If a child is rejected and disrespected by her classmates, or if she is discouraged by her parents or teachers, she will develop feelings of inadequacy and worthlessness.

Linda Rubin reports that low self-esteem has been found to have a significant correlation with psychiatric assistance, depression, and aggressive behaviors in children. She also found that there is a strong relationship between low self-esteem and anxiety. Symptoms of this anxiety are nervousness, loss of appetite, insomnia, headaches, and reduced task performance.

If female students continue to be short-changed in their education, and if schools continue to allow them to be demeaned and harassed by their fellow classmates, it is very likely that they will develop an unstable self-image. Rosenberg believes that people with low self-esteem tend to present "false fronts" as a way to cope with feelings of worthlessness. This is understandable because females receive conflicting messages at school and in the community. On one hand, the media and many parents and educators tell females that they are equal to boys and they can do anything they want to do with their lives. On the other hand, sexual harassment makes many females unsure of themselves and unable to control their lives.

Rosenberg has shown that social classification based on sex can profoundly effect a person's sense of identity. If students attend a school where a ride on a school bus or walk down the hall might result in being insulted and humiliated, their self- esteem will be significantly and negatively impacted.

Common physical complaints resulting from sexual harassment include headaches and ulcers. When a student is sexually harassed and nothing is done to stop the harassment, more serious stress-related diseases can develop. A student under very high stress may become unable to function normally.

But there is even more. There is fear, anger, and depression. Research indicates that women suffer twice as many depressive disorders as men. While we can't attribute the incidence of these depressive disorders solely to sexual harassment, we strongly believe there is a significant correlation, particularly in regard to adolescent females. It should not surprise us that a young woman faced with unrelenting abuse might find the circumstances of her life quite depressing, and depression is significantly associated with suicide and suicide attempts. It is also fitting to note here that females attempt suicide three times more often than do males.

Behavioral Consequences

Although they were discussing sexual discrimination on college campuses (rather than in elementary and secondary schools), Roberta Hall and Bernice Sandler found classrooms to have a "chilly" climate for women. They state: "Whether overt or subtle, differential treatment based on sex is far from innocuous. Its cumulative effects can be damaging not only to individual women and men students but also to the educational process." According to Hall and Sandler, this type of climate has a profound negative impact on females' academic and career development by:

√   discouraging classroom participation;

√   preventing students from seeking help outside of class;

√   causing students to drop or avoid certain classes, to switch major or subspecialities within majors, and in some instances even to leave a given institution;

√   minimizing the development of individual collegial relationships with faculty which are crucial for future professional development.

√   dampening career aspirations; and

√   undermining confidence.

A chilly climate may also result in causing women to believe and act as though:

√   their presence in a given class, department, program or institution is at best peripheral, or at worst an unwelcome intrusion;

√   their participation in class discussion is not expected, and their contributions are not important;

√   their capacity for full intellectual development and professional success is limited; and

√   their academic and career goals are not matters for serious attention or concern.

Although women students are the most directly harmed by an inhospitable climate, Hall and Sandler believe that male students are also affected. "If limited views of women are overtly or subtly communicated by faculty, some men students may experience reinforcement of their own negative views about women especially because such views are confirmed by persons of knowledge and status. This will result in men having a difficult time seeing women as full peers with whom to work and collaborate and support as colleagues.

The AAUW documents the following additional behavioral consequences for victims of sexual harassment; avoiding the person(s) who harassed them, staying away from particular places in the school or on the school grounds, changing their seats in class, stopping attendance at a particular activity or sport, changing their group of friends, and changing the way they come to or go home from school.

Educational Consequences

The AAUW study of sexual harassment in schools was the first to attempt to determine how sexual harassment affects students educationally, emotionally, and behaviorally. The findings of this study clearly indicate that a hostile environment significantly impacts the lives of students and demonstrates that sexual harassment in our schools is significantly hurting female students' chances for success in school. The most frequent consequence of sexual harassment was to cause the victim to "not want to go to school" (33 percent). This outcome was followed by; "not wanting to talk as much in class" (32 percent), "finding it hard to pay attention in school" (28 percent), "staying home from school or cutting a class" (24 percent), "making a lower grade on a test paper" (23 percent), "finding it hard to study" (22 percent), "making a lower grade in class" (20 percent), "thinking about changing schools" (18 percent), and "doubting whether you have what it takes to graduate from high school" (5 percent). Three percent of the students in this study said that they had actually changed schools as a result of sexual harassment.

Chapter Four

Legal Aspects of Sexual Harassment

The Function of Laws and Courts

In the hope of achieving harmony the majority of us voluntarily allows laws to regulate our behavior. Lawmakers and judges are involved in the constant process of attempting to strike a balance that allows individuals as much freedom as possible while at the same time protecting the rights of others. The Constitution protects our individual rights while various state and federal laws protect the general welfare of society and implement the constitutional protection of individuals.

Laws are not made in isolation from what is happening in society. As society changes and new relationships evolve, new laws are needed to respond to the new view of what is right and what is wrong. As groups of people request or demand legal protection, public opinion interacts with lawmaking to ensure that new laws reflect the values of the majority. Consequently, laws both shape and reflect the values of society.

Because our society is made up of people who hold many different values, new rules are not accepted by everyone at the same rate. Some people are way out in front of a value shift. They are the people who are fighting for a new idea before most of us understand what they are talking about. For example, Farley coined the term sexual harassment in 1974, but it wasn't until 1986 that the Supreme Court ruled that sexual harassment was a form of sex discrimination. By the time a new idea is formalized into law, most people have formed an opinion about it, and the majority of the people accept the new law. However, there are always people who continue to fight against a new value, even after it is passed into law. They keep testing the resolve of society to uphold the new law. Some of this testing takes place in private actions and some takes place in the courts.

The current confusion about the legal status of sexual harassment is an example of the complex process of translating a new value into new rules for behavior. While some people are fighting to gain equal treatment for women, others are resisting any change in the role and status of women. When there are conflicting beliefs about appropriate and inappropriate behavior, courts are asked to resolve the controversy. The process is further confused by the fact that judges, as part of society, have their own sets of values. Therefore, each judge interprets the law through his or her own set of values.

Laws are society's attempt to ensure that consequences will result if certain prohibited acts are committed. Courts were created to interpret the laws and to ensure that all citizens are treated equally and judged by the same standards of behavior when consequences are meted out. The overall purpose of laws and the court system is to produce solidarity, continuity, and conformity within society. The end result of all law is justice.

Because no law can specifically describe all possible actions, we don't know exactly which specific behaviors are legal and which are illegal until a court makes a ruling on the specific facts of a case. Therefore, the court system has a major influence on all of our behavior. As our attitudes toward women have evolved, courts have been called upon to provide clarification regarding women's legal rights. For a long time courts reinforced society's paternalistic belief that "a woman's place was in the home." By looking at a few of these court decisions we will be able to see that there has been a gradual shift in the courts' view of women.

One of the most famous cases which illustrates a paternalistic view of women is the 1872 case of *Bradwell v. Illinois.* In this decision the U.S. Supreme Court upheld the Illinois Supreme Court's refusal to allow women to practice law. In his concurring opinion Justice Bradley wrote, "Man is or should be woman's protector and defender...the natural and proper timidity and delicacy which belong to the female sex evidently unfits it for many of the occupations of civil life...the paramount destiny and mission of women are to fulfill the noble and benign offices of wife and mother."

Thirty years later, in the case of *Muller v. Oregon*, the U. S. Supreme Court affirmed a decision that restricted the number of hours that a woman could work during any one day on the grounds that "...history discloses the fact that woman has always been dependent upon man...it cannot be denied that she still looks to her brother and depends upon him. The reason rests on the inherent difference between the two sexes, and in the different functions in life which they perform."

As recently as 1966, in the case of *State v. Hall,* a Mississippi court upheld a state statute that excluded women from serving on juries. The court stated that women should be excluded so that "they may continue their service as mothers, wives, and homemakers, and so to protect them from the filth, obscenity, and obnoxious atmosphere that so often pervades a courtroom during a jury trial."

In a 1973 case that involved secondary school students, a state court ruled that girls could be excluded from a high school cross-country running team because, "Athletic competition builds character in boys. We don't need that kind of character in our girls, the women of tomorrow."

Sexual Harassment is Against the Law

In the late 1960s and early 1970s concerned teachers, students and parents began to struggle against sex bias and discrimination in our nations schools. This awareness and commitment resulted in the passage of Title IX of the Education Amendments of 1972.

It has only been in the last decade that courts have clearly placed women under the protection of the U.S. Constitution. Although it is now well established that sexual harassment is sexual discrimination, this understanding is still evolving. The definition of sexual harassment not only changes from situation to situation, but from case to case, and from court to court.

The earliest sexual harassment cases came from events that took place in the workplace, later cases emerged from colleges and universities, and recently many sexual harassment cases are originating in elementary and secondary schools.⁾

Lower courts and the U. S. Supreme Court are gradually clarifying the legal status of sexual harassment. Each new case provides more clarity as to what constitutes sexual harassment. As a result of court action, the Equal Employment Opportunity Commission regulations on sexual harassment have been upheld as a lawful regulatory interpretation of Title VII of the Civil Rights Act of 1964, and that sexual harassment is a violation of Title IX of the Education Amendments of 1972.

As a direct result of the Senate confirmation hearings of Judge Clarence Thomas, Congress enacted the Civil Rights Act of 1991 for the express purpose of providing "additional remedies under federal law...to deter unlawful harassment." By providing for compensatory and punitive damages relating to punishment and providing a trial by jury, this act actually encourages suits charging sexual harassment. In addition to the back pay, front pay, reinstatement, and attorneys' fees previously available under Title VII, this act authorizes as much as $300,000 in compensatory damages.

The law regarding sexual harassment of students in less clear than harassment of adults for several reasons. Problems arise because most of the victims and harassers are minors, and our legal system has a difficult time evaluating both harm and responsibility when minors are involved. Although she was referring to college students when she made the following comments, Laurie LeClair's comments are also relevant to elementary and secondary school students. She identifies three factors that add to the courts' confusion. They are (1) students are more likely than employees to be transient, and consequently their interest in institutional reform tends to be short lived, (2) students lack financial incentives to pursue litigation, and (3) courts are more reluctant to intervene in the academic context than in the non-academic context.

The laws that govern sexual harassment of elementary and secondary school teachers are the same as those that affect all public, federally funded entities. For example, whether you are an office worker or a fourth grade teacher, you are protected from discrimination by Title VII of the Civil Rights Act and section 1983 of the United States Code. This law is enforced by the Equal Employment Opportunity Commission (EEOC), a federal agency.

Public school students are protected by Title IX of the Education Amendments of 1972. Title IX is one of the most sweeping sex discrimination laws ever passed. Although it had little early enforcement, it is now the primary tool that defines equal educational opportunity for women in schools. Under Title IX, sexual harassment is defined as *"verbal or physical conduct of a sexual nature, imposed on the basis of sex, by an employee or agent of a recipient that denies, limits, provides different, or conditions the provision of aid, benefits, services or treatment protected under Title IX."*

In addition to criminal charges (assault, battery, rape, etc.), because sexual harassment often involves unsolicited, offensive, physical touching and psychological and emotional harm, victims of sexual harassment can bring additional state law civil claims against the harasser. This type of claim for redress of a civil wrong is known as a tort. These tort claims include assault, battery, and intentional infliction of emotional distress.

Sexual Harassment Continuum

As we look at the various behaviors on this continuum we must remember that in order for any of these behaviors to be considered sexual harassment they must be unwanted. We can also see that as we move to the right on the continuum the behaviors become progressively more serious. At the left of the continuum are behaviors that must occur frequently and persistently in order for them to be strictly considered as sexual harassment. However, as we move to the right the behaviors become more severe. Just one incident at the right half of the continuum would probably be considered sexual harassment. For example, staring at a woman's breasts, vaginal area or buttocks is clearly rude. However, it must occur persistently and flagrantly to be considered sexual harassment. On the other hand, even one incident of solicitation of sexual activity by a teacher is sexual harassment. And any unwanted physical touching or physical assault is considered sexual harassment as well as a violation of other statutory protections.

In addition to federal protection, most states have civil rights statutes which govern discrimination, including sexual harassment. Some state civil rights statutes have general prohibitions against sexual discrimination. However, states such as Connecticut specifically define sexual harassment as a "discriminatory employment practice." Although most of the current law relating to sexual harassment developed from cases where the victims of the harassment were adults, more recent cases involve elementary and secondary school students. California, Illinois, Iowa, Minnesota, and Wisconsin have statutes that specifically prohibit sexual harassment in schools. For example, all Minnesota schools are currently required to have written sexual harassment policies. These policies must include rules and consequences that are posted in the schools and included in student handbooks. All athletic and extra-curricular programs must have a specific policy against sexual harassment and violence.

In 1993 Minnesota Attorney General Hubert Humphrey III conducted a state wide survey to determine the impact and level of compliance with the Minnesota sexual harassment statute. The results of the survey are discouraging. According to Humphrey, "While all responding schools said they have developed written policies, only 38 percent believe their policy is well understood by students and staff." Humphrey believes that training and education are essential to ensure that students and staff clearly understand what harassment is, who to report to, and what the consequences are. It is interesting to note that although the survey was completed by superintendents, principals or guidance counselors, 12 percent didn't know if their students were required to attend the training sessions. On the next page is a chart that shows how sexual harassment in elementary and secondary schools occurs on a continuum, ranging from environmental to *quid pro quo* to physical force.

Sexual Harassment Continuum

ENVIRONMENTAL VISUAL	ENVIRONMENTAL WRITTEN	ENVIRONMENTAL VERBAL	ENVIRONMENTAL PHYSICAL	QUID PRO QUO VERBAL	PHYSICAL FORCE
•Staring	•Magazines	•Sexual innuendoes	•Standing "too close"	•Pressure for dates	•Physical corrosion for sex
•Ogling	•Flyers	•Using sexist, derogatory language	•Brushing against	•Pressure for sex	•Physical assault
•Obscene gestures	•Graffiti	•Unwanted requests for dates	•Touching	•Unwanted phone calls	•Rape
•Mooning	•Cartoons	•Lewd comments	•Patting	•Implied threats of retaliation	
•Simulating masturbation	•Photos	•Insulting sounds	•Grabbing	•Overt threats of retaliation	
•Simulating intercourse	•Posters	•"Dirty"/sexual jokes	•Pinching		
	•Obscene fax messages	•Questions about personal life	•Caressing		
	•Obscene e-mail	•Comments about body	•Kissing		
	•Obscene poems	•Spreading rumors	•Touching hair		
	•Unwanted notes		•Fondling		
	•Unwanted letters		•"Flipping" skirt up		
			•Stalking		
			•Coerced sex		

© 1993 Shoop and Hayhow, used by permission.

What is Sexual Harassment

Over the past ten years most sexual harassment cases have been based upon the *EEOC Guidelines on Discrimination Because of Sex*. According to these guidelines, unwelcome sexual advances, requests for sexual favors, and other verbal or physical conduct of a sexual nature is sexual harassment if; (1) submission to such conduct is made either explicitly or implicitly a term or condition of an individual's employment, (2) submission to or rejection of such conduct by an individual is used as the basis for employment decisions affecting such individual, or (3) such conduct has the purpose or effect of unreasonably interfering with an individual's work performance or creating an intimidating, hostile, or offensive working environment. The first two subsections of the EEOC guidelines define *quid pro quo* harassment. The third subsection describes environmental sexual harassment. A subset of the hostile work environment is known as sexual favoritism.

Quid pro quo, environmental, and sexual favoritism sexual harassment regularly occur in our elementary and secondary schools. Although it is sometimes difficult to distinguish between the categories, it is important to do so because school districts are held to different standards for each.

Sexual activity between two consenting adults is not illegal in the workplace. Such sexual activity is not sexual harassment unless it is unwanted. However, sexual activity between an adult and a minor student is always illegal. Sexual activity between a teacher and a student, or propositions for such activity are grounds for dismissal and for criminal action against the teacher.

Because of the special relationship between the school and the student, schools have a duty to protect students from sexual abuse by teachers. In addition to violating criminal law, a teacher having sex with a student is also a form of *quid pro quo* sexual harassment. Because this type of behavior is covered by criminal law, we will not discuss it in detail, other than to say that schools are liable for *quid pro quo* harassment regardless of whether or not the school knew about the harassment.

Whether it takes place in the workplace or the school, environmental sexual harassment is not as easy to identify. Therefore, schools are usually liable only if the school knew or should have known of the harassment and did not take adequate steps to prevent it.

Just as most parents are not aware that their daughters are being sexually harassed in school, many teachers and administrators are also unaware of the extent of the problem. This does not mean that they do not see the behavior, they simply do not recognize that it is illegal. Boys have been behaving inappropriately toward girls for so long that it is often accepted as the norm. The following two events were reported to us this year by elementary school teachers.

> *"During recess at an elementary school two or three boys pick out one girl they really like. The boys chase the girl, catch her, and each boy takes a turn giving the 'girl of his dreams' a kiss on her mouth."*

> *"During recess boys pick out one girl and chase after her. After catching her, one of the boys pulls down her pants. Then all the boys run away and start after another girl."*

If you think back to your own elementary school days, you can probably remember an event similar to one of the above. You might have even participated in such an activity. Does the event bring a smile to your face or does it bring memories of pain? We recently asked a group of high school girls to tell us about incidents from their past that they now thought might have been examples of sexual harassment. One girl quietly said, "Please don't ask me to talk about this. It makes me too sad." Before you discount her reaction as being overly sensitive, ask yourself how you react to the following story, told to us by the parent of the girl involved.

> *"My daughter attended a high school football game with a group of girl friends. As she was coming back from the bathroom a group of boys jumped her and pulled her to the ground. They pulled her sweatshirt and bra up around her neck and wrote their names on her chest with magic markers. What really hurt her the most was that these boys were her friends. They said they were 'just fooling around.'"*

Regardless of how you remember your school days, or how you personally react to the above stories, today each of these events are examples of sexual harassment. Clearly, the rules have changed. What may have been acceptable behavior even a short time ago is now considered sexual harassment. Many teachers and administrators are not aware of this change and they do not understand that they are responsible for seeing that sexual harassment does not take place in their schools. Consequently most schools have done little or nothing to stop sexual harassment of students.

Just as 1986 is remembered as the year that the U. S. Supreme Court ruled sexual harassment is an illegal form of sex discrimination, 1992 will be remembered as the year when educators were informed that sexual harassment of students is also an illegal form of sex discrimination. The U. S. Supreme Court made it clear that schools owe their students protection from sexual harassment by teachers and by other students.

Schools must act in a pro-active manner to eradicate sexual harassment. Whether subtle or overt, sexual harassment is categorized as either *quid pro quo*, sexual favoritism, or hostile educational environment. However, many educators still do not recognize or understand the extent or seriousness of the problem. Let's look at the three categories of sexual harassment in the context of a school environment.

Quid Pro Quo

Quid pro quo sexual harassment is the easiest type of harassment to recognize. It occurs when sexual demands are made upon a student in exchange for educational participation, advancement, or other benefits. Even one such incident is *quid pro quo* sexual harassment. Because of the age and vulnerability of students, even if the female student "welcomes" the sexual attention, the school is liable for sexual harassment and the offending teacher is liable for sexual harassment as well as other criminal charges.

Although *quid pro quo* harassment is clearly a violation of Title IX, some courts have drawn a distinction between standard and retaliatory *quid pro quo*. Standard *quid pro quo* harassment involves expressed or implied demands for sexual favors in return for some benefit, such as a grade, special treatment, or a letter of reference. Retaliatory *quid pro quo* exists when a teacher makes sexual advances to a student without either expressing or implying that the student will be affected by a refusal. It becomes sexual harassment if, upon being refused, the teacher then makes life miserable for the student. The distinction between standard and retaliatory *quid pro quo* is usually not significant because both categories are classified as sexual harassment.

Sexual Favoritism

Sexual favoritism is also fairly easy to identify. It occurs when a student receives benefits as a result of his or her submission to the teacher's sexual advances or requests for sexual favors. The victims of the harassment are the other students in the class who are treated unfairly because they are not objects of the teacher's romantic interest. In the workplace, this type of sexual harassment has resulted in successful law suits brought on behalf of qualified persons who were denied employment opportunities or benefits. However, courts have required proof of the sexual relationship, not merely rumors or innuendos. Courts have yet to offer consistent views on how to treat sexual harassment cases in which a student is favored by a teacher who has a romantic interest in her.

Hostile Educational Environment

In the workplace this is called hostile work environment sexual harassment, in a school setting we will call this a hostile educational environment. Hostile educational environment is the form of sexual harassment that is the most confusing to many people. This form of harassment is less tangible, less discrete, and often occurs over a period of time. Unlike *quid pro quo* and sexual favoritism harassment, which may involve a single incident, sexually hostile or intimidating environments are characterized by multiple, varied, and frequent occurrences.

What Constitutes A Hostile Educational Environment

In the school setting the hostile educational environment theory is based on the assumption that the relationship between the student and the school is very significant and that students should be protected from psychological as well as physical abuse. Each student should be able to come to school free from fear and free from harm.

In a case where an elementary school girl complained to the school after an elementary school boy used extremely graphic and abusive sexual language on the school bus, the school principal and several parents said that the boy's behavior was inappropriate, but that it was not sexual harassment. They argued that in order for sexual harassment to exist the offending student must have a sophisticated understanding of sexuality, and must have intended the behavior to be sexual. This argument demonstrates a lack of understanding of sexual harassment. The *intent* of the harasser is irrelevant. It is the *impact* of the action that determines whether or not sexual harassment has taken place.

In order for a behavior to be considered to have created a hostile educational environment, four elements must exist. First, the harassment must be based on a person's sex. (It will be unlikely that a court will find behavior that is equally offensive to men and women to be sexual harassment.) This does not mean that a school cannot prohibit such behavior, but a victim will probably not succeed in a sexual harassment suit. Second, the sexual behavior must be unwelcome to the victim. The victim must not have solicited or incited the offensive behavior, and the victim must regard the conduct as undesirable or offensive. If a female student engages in sexual banter and frequently uses sexual innuendos, she may have a difficult time convincing a judge that later, more offensive behavior is sexual harassment. Third, the offensive behavior must be sufficiently severe or pervasive to alter conditions of the school climate and create a hostile educational environment. One off-color joke or comment will usually not be considered to be sexual harassment. And fourth, in order for the school to be liable for sexual harassment, the school district must have known or should have known of the harassment and failed to take prompt, effective, remedial action. Because the school district is expected to control the educational environment, it is held responsible for sexual harassment (see chart on next page).

Some people are confused about the hostile educational environment in schools, because in many cases the harasser is a student who has no formal, recognized authority over the victim. Secondly, because student victims of sexual harassment often have no obvious loss or physical injury, some people do not recognize that an injury has occurred. And finally, much of the behavior that female students find offensive is behavior that has long been accepted as normal heterosexual behavior by many men and boys. It must be remembered that schools are liable for sexual harassment if the behavior creates an intimidating, offensive or hostile environment regardless of any other impact on the students.

Elements of a Hostile Educational Environment

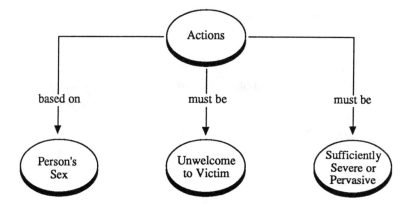

Harassment by A Fellow Student

In the *Meritor* decision, the U.S. Supreme Court ruled that sexual harassment violates Title VII if it creates a hostile or offensive environment for the victim, regardless of whether it threatened the individual's job. Although the *Meritor* decision was based on Title VII, Title IX cases will likely follow the same judicial reasoning. In the school setting, this means that student initiated unwelcome sexual advances, requests for sexual favors, and other verbal or physical conduct of a sexual nature constitute sexual harassment. A key question is whether the sexual advances were unwelcome.

Remarks that simply offend a person's feelings are usually not sexual harassment. However, if the offending behavior is severe or pervasive enough to actually affect a student's educational environment, then it is sexual harassment. In this context there is a clear difference between welcome and voluntary. For example, even if an alleged victim agreed to participate in sexual intimacy, the sexual advances are a prohibited form of sexual harassment if it is clear that the victim did not desire to have the sexual relationship, but capitulated under pressure.

The Concept of Welcomeness

Because the 1980 EEOC guidelines do not define "unwelcome," we must look to various court cases in order to understand the difference between a voluntary activity and a welcome activity. In the *Meritor* case the victim claimed that she initially refused the sexual advances of her supervisor, but she eventually gave in and engaged in sexual intercourse out of fear of losing her job. The Supreme Court ruled that her participation in a sexual relationship did not establish that the relationship was truly consensual or welcome. The Court ruled that "the fact that the sex-related conduct was voluntary, in the sense that the complainant was not forced to participate against her will, is not a defense to a sexual harassment suit brought under Title VII." The court in the 1982 case of *Henson v. City of Dundee*, provided a general definition of welcomeness that has been followed by many other courts. Challenged conduct must be unwelcome "in the sense that the employee did not solicit or incite it, and in the sense that the employee regarded the conduct as undesirable or offensive."

In 1990 the EEOC issued its *Policy Guidance on Current Issues of Sexual Harassment.* These guidelines instructed that when there is conflicting evidence of welcomeness, "the record as a whole and the totality of the circumstances," should be used to evaluate on a case by case basis. EEOC suggests that if there is a complaint of unwelcome sexual attention, the complaint is strengthened if it is made immediately after the event.

Severe or Pervasive

How much sexual harassment must a student endure before she has a case that will hold up in court? The EEOC has consistently ruled that "sexual flirtation or innuendo, even vulgar language that is trivial or merely annoying, will not usually be considered a violation of law." For example, if a male student calls a female student a "bitch" after a disagreement, it may be rude, it may be inappropriate, but it is probably not sexual harassment. Although probably not sexual harassment, this does not mean that a school should approve or permit such offensive behavior. However, if the above mentioned boy follows the girl down the hall shouting obscenities at her, writes vulgar comments about her on the bathroom walls, and spreads sexual rumors about her, then the behavior is then sufficiently pervasive and severe to qualify as sexual harassment.

Reasonableness

Courts will find a person liable for sexual harassment if the actions are unwelcome, and if there is a pattern of severe or pervasive behavior. In light of the above discussion, it is logical to ask, "What standard does the court use to make this determination?" Until recently, the basis for finding that a behavior is sufficiently severe or pervasive to constitute sexual harassment was the objective standard of "reasonableness." Historically this test question asked whether a "reasonable person," under the victim's circumstances, would consider the action to be hostile. Early courts looked at the behavior to determine if it "would have interfered with a reasonable individual's work performance."

Although the EEOC's guidelines support the reasonable person test, recent court decisions indicate that courts are becoming aware of the gender hierarchy that shapes much of the interaction between women and men in the workplace and at school. That is, women and men often interpret the same behavior differently.

Circuit Judge Beezer stated that if the reasonable person standards were accepted, victims of sexual harassment would have to endure the harassment until their psychological well-being was seriously affected to the extent that they suffered anxiety and debilitation before they could establish a hostile environment. He said that sexual harassment falls somewhere between forcible rape and the mere utterance of an epithet. "Although an isolated epithet by itself fails to support a cause of action for a hostile environment,

Title VII's protection of employees from sex discrimination should come into play long before the point where victims of sexual harassment require psychiatric assistance."

The danger in using the reasonable person test when it is clear that boys and girls see the same situation differently can be illustrated by listening to how some boys view sexual harassment. When asked to view video taped scenes of various forms of sexual harassment, boys often recognize that the girl in the scene is offended by the behavior, but they make comments such as "That's just the way boys are," or "I don't see the problem, the boys were just joking," or "if the girls don't like the way boys talk or behave they should not go into classes or jobs that are 'men's' work."

In evaluating a hostile educational environment, the focus should be on the perspective of the victim. Using the "reasonable person" standard runs the risk of reinforcing the prevailing level of discrimination (i.e., if men and women see things differently, and courts continued to use the reasonable man test, then it would be unlikely that women would win many sexual harassment cases.) Men and boys could continue to harass merely because a particular discriminatory practice was common, and women and girls would have no remedy. There is a broad range of view-points among women as a group, of course, but many women share common concerns which men do not. A "reasonable person" standard tends to be male-biased and ignores the experiences of women.

Beezer states that "by acknowledging and not trivializing the effects of sexual harassment on a 'reasonable woman,' courts can work towards ensuring that neither men nor women will have to 'run a gauntlet of sexual abuse' in return for the privilege of being allowed to work and make a living."

Courts have held that "the objective standard asks whether a reasonable person of the same sex as the victim, that is, a reasonable woman, would perceive that an abusive working environment has been created." In schools this means that the concept of psychological well-being is measured by the impact of the school environment on a "reasonable female" student's school performance or more broadly by the impact of the stress inflicted on her by the continuing presence of the harassing behavior. The fact that some female students do not complain of the school environment or find some behaviors objectionable does not mean that the school environment as a whole is not offensive.

In light of the above discussion, one point must be clarified. Just because men and women may interpret each others behaviors differently, it does not mean that intimidating, hostile or offensive educational environments are simply the result of differences of perceptions. In the *Sparks* case, the court stated that "the whole point of sexual harassment claims is that behavior that may be permissible in some settings can be abusive in the workplace." This means that behavior that may occur in a person's home or in his or her social life is not sexual harassment, regardless of how rude or offensive it is. However, that same behavior on a school bus or in the school building may be grounds for charges of sexual harassment.

Taxonomy of Sexual Harassment

Throughout our discussion we have focused on student-to-student sexual harassment, primarily male students harassing female students. As we stated earlier, we did this because the impact of sexual harassment is greater on females than it is on males, and in

95% of reported cases the harasser is a fellow student. However, other forms of sexual harassment certainly exist. They include: 1) teacher-to-student, 2) harassment of males, 3) harassment of gay and lesbian students, 4) student-to-teacher, 5) group harassment, and 5) harassment by non-employees. The chart on the next page depicts the various types of sexual harassment.

Sexual Harassment: Who Does it Affect?

Students → can inflict → Sexual Harassment

Teachers → can inflict → Sexual Harassment

Administrators → can inflict → Sexual Harassment

Classified Employees → can inflict → Sexual Harassment

Non-Employees → can inflict → Sexual Harassment

Sexual Harassment → on → Student → can inflict → Sexual Harassment

Sexual Harassment → on → Students

Sexual Harassment → on → Teachers

Sexual Harassment → on → Administrators

Sexual Harassment → on → Classified Employees

Sexual Harassment → on → Non-Employees

Student-to-Student Sexual Harassment

Peer sexual harassment is the newest form of sexual harassment to be recognized by the courts. Evidence presented in a 1992 study conducted by the American Association of University Women (AAUW) documents that boys do not treat girls very well in our schools. Reports of unwelcome verbal and physical behavior of a sexual nature imposed by boys on girls in elementary, middle school and high schools are increasing. The AAUW report indicates that far too many school authorities do not view this as a serious occurrence and treat the behavior as an example of "boys being boys." Because of this unchecked behavior on the part of boys, many girls are reluctant to enroll in courses where they may be the only female.

Schools that do not stop peer sexual harassment may be liable to their students. During 1992 several school districts were held liable for the sexual harassment of students by other students. John Lewis, Susan Hastings and Anne Morgan report that an eighth grade student sued a San Francisco school district and her principal for unchecked peer harassment. The student alleged that boys repeatedly yelled "moo moo" and made vulgar references to her breasts and other body parts. The school district settled by paying the student $20,000. In another case, a Minnesota student charged her school district with sexual harassment for failing to remove graffiti that called her a "slut" and made other sexual comments about her. This school district settled the case for $15,000.

In April of 1993, the Chaska, Minnesota school district agreed to pay $40,000 to a former high school student to settle a complaint stemming from sexual harassment she suffered while in school. According to an article in *Education Week*, "this settlement is believed to be the largest nationwide to date in a student-to-student sexual harassment case." This case involved a complaint filed with the state human-rights department when the student discovered that her name was on a list circulated at the school that described her as sexually desirable and contained lewd and sexually graphic descriptions. School officials denied a request that the incident be used as a lesson on sexual harassment. Instead, they offered her counseling. The department ruled that the school district did not take timely and appropriate action on student-to-student sexual harassment.

Sexual harassment cases are not just occurring in our high schools. In a case that received a great deal of national media attention, a 7-year-old girl accused little boys of sexually harassing her on the school bus in Eden Prairie, Minnesota. In her complaint she stated that she was subjected to "multiple or severe acts" of harassment, including name-calling and unwelcome touching. According to Roger Murphey, public affairs officer for the Education Department, "the acts of sexual harassment were not confined to the school bus. It happened in the classroom, in the hallways, on the playground." In May of 1993 she won a historic battle when federal investigators concluded that her civil rights were violated by the school district. The case is the first in the United States involving student-to-student harassment among elementary age students. After a seven-month probe, the U.S. Department of Education's Office For Civil Rights accused the district of failing to respond properly to a "sexually hostile environment." Although the district did not admit any wrongdoing, it entered into a settlement with the federal government in which it agreed to be more vigilant in fighting sexual harassment.

A particularly interesting aspect of the school district's defense was their contention that they were obliged to treat some of the harassers more gently because they were emotionally disturbed students who qualify for special education under federal law. The Office for Civil Rights rejected this argument. In the letter of finding the Office for Civil Rights said, "The rights of students with disabilities may not operate as defense of behavior which singles out students, because of their sex, for adverse consequences."

One of the more important points in this case was made by Sue Sattel, sex equity specialist with the Minnesota Department of Education when she said, "The Office For Civil Rights is saying children don't even have to know what sex is to be sexually harassed. It's more about demeaning and degrading and making a hostile and intimidating environment."

Lewis, Hastings and Morgan report that a case is pending in Illinois where a girl's parents are seeking compensation for private school tuition and the costs of their child's counseling because third-grade elementary students pinched their daughter's chest, groin and buttocks on several occasions.

The number of cases alleging sexual harassment between peers in elementary and secondary schools is increasing. Although it is still too early to be able to define with certainty what courts will determine to be sexual harassment, it is clear that when a student is being harassed on the basis of his or her sex, it is sexual harassment.

Teacher-to-Student Sexual Harassment

Because most sexual harassment in schools is student-to-student harassment, we have spent most of our time discussing this type of harassment. However, it is important to recognize that sexual abuse and violent intimidation of students by school employees as well as sexual harassment of students by teachers is a very serious problem. During the past few years there have been hundreds of reported incidents of sexual abuse of students by teachers and other school employees. William Valente notes that "this alarming increase in reported cases of sexual molestation of public school students by teachers has sensitized everyone to the need for improved monitoring and control measures."

According to Valente "student molestation claims have centered on the argument that school districts and school superiors have a federal law duty to protect students from sexual abuse by teachers." He reports that in the case of *Stoneking v. Bradford Area School Dist.,* the court decided that compulsory education statutes and the common law of Pennsylvania imposed a constitutional duty to the school to investigate and take reasonable steps to protect the students who were subjected to ongoing sexual assault and molestation by a school employee. On remand the court ruled that schools could be held liable for deliberate indifference by school authorities to the deprivation of a student's constitutional right to bodily security.

The relationship between teachers and students is a special one, therefore teachers will be held to a higher standard of care under common law than are other employees. The previously mentioned case of *Franklin v. Gwinnett County Public Schools* raised the stakes for schools. The U. S. Supreme Court made it clear that schools must handle promptly and effectively complaints concerning sexual misconduct of school employees. This decision made it clear that Title IX is available to students who to seek to recover damages against a school district for sexual the misconduct of its employees. Schools have been put on notice that they must not only investigate complaints of sexual misconduct after the incident has allegedly occurred, but they must also institute preventative measures to protect students and employees from future harassment.

Often charges pertaining to school employee dismissal involving sexual misconduct involves criminal as well as civil issues. Not only may a school employee be terminated from their employment, but they may be charged in a criminal court. According to Ralph Mawdsley and Frederick Hampton the traditional standard for determining innocence in a civil case is the preponderance of evidence, and in a criminal case evidence beyond a reasonable doubt.

The National Association of Secondary School Principals (NASSP) reminds us that although "in many states, under statutes or collective bargaining agreements, certain categories of employees cannot be discharged without demonstration that the alleged unacceptable conduct is irremediable, but irremediability has not been a serious prohibition to discharging employees for sexual misconduct with students."

Sexual misconduct of school employees involving students has been treated seriously and severely by the courts. Mawdsley and Hampton suggest that the that courts virtual unanimous support of the dismissal of school employees for sexual misconduct combined with the impact of the *Gwinnett* decision may produce a surge of lawsuits against school districts for the sexual misconduct of school personnel. These suits will likely be based on sexual harassment in the form of "verbal comments, physical contact, and appearances of impropriety."

They suggest that schools: 1) limit physical conduct of employees with student to situations where health or safety are factors, 2) publish punishments for inappropriate physical conduct, including notice of hearing rights under statute or collective bargaining agreement, 3) encourage students to report all physical contact to appropriate school officials, and 5) establish a time frame to investigate complaints, including the name of the person who will conduct the investigation.

Many incidents of teacher-to-student sexual abuse are not reported. Too often the offending teacher is given the option of resigning and the tragic event is never reported. These teachers have been allowed to move to another town and repeat the abuse with other students. Fortunately, what was once referred to as "unprofessional conduct" is now being correctly prosecuted as sexual assault or rape.

Philip Villaume and Michael Foley identify three kinds of student sexual abuse. The first is inappropriate sexual contact with a student's intimate body parts, such as breasts, genitals, inner thigh, and buttocks. The second type is that of a sexual relationship between a student and an educator, and the third is sexual harassment of a student by an educator.

Although the offending teacher can be male or female, most of the cases we are familiar with involve male teachers and female students. Quite often these relationships are sexual relations in which the teacher alleges that the student willingly initiated the relationship or was a willing partner. Any sexual contact between a teacher and a student is an outrageous violation of professional standards and common decency and should never be condoned or tolerated. Although there is currently a national debate raging regarding sexual relationships between college students and professors, there is no debate about the impropriety and illegality of sexual relationships between teachers and students.

Discharge for sexual relations with students may even extend beyond the time the student attends the school. The NASSP reports that in the case of *Sertik v. School Board of Pittsburgh* a teacher who had sexual intercourse with a student during the student's last semester in high school was discovered by police having intercourse with the same student during the summer following the student's graduation. The court upheld the discharge because of "the School District's interest in its students of relatively tender years and insuring an appropriate school environment..."

Courts have even upheld the dismissal of a teacher for student allegations regarding sexual misconduct that were raised years after the conduct. The NASSP reports that in the case of *Johnson v. Independent School District No. 294* the discharge of a teacher for having sexual intercourse with a 16-year-old student was upheld four years after the incident took place. In this case the court commented that "by virtue of the nature of the offense, sexual intercourse with a minor student of the district, it may be considered doubtful whether such conduct could ever be too remote in time."

Teacher-to-student sexual harassment takes all of the forms discussed in the student-to-student section. The NASSP reports that discharges have been upheld for: a school bus driver who touched, grabbed, hugged, kissed, and lay on female pupil passengers; a planetarium technician who kissed one student; a teacher who pinched three second grade girls on the buttocks during P.E. class; a third grade teacher who was involved in two fondling incidents with 9-year-old girls; a teacher who touched the thigh of a fifth grade female student, making rubbing movement and causing the girl to run crying to the office; a band teacher who improperly touched and kissed three sixth and seventh grade female students; a band teacher who struck three male students lightly on the genitals; a P.E. coach who hugged female students against their will and who slapped at least one student on the buttocks and placed his hand on the knee of another; a teacher who twice held a 12-year-old emotionally disturbed male student in his lap and rocked and kissed the boy; a teacher of the perceptually-impaired who showed sexually explicit materials to her students; a teacher who hugged, kissed, and touched five female students; and a science teacher who kissed and fondled a female student in the science preparation room several times during one year.

Verbal comments that have sexual connotation are also grounds for teacher dismissal. According to the NASSP courts seem very supportive of school district efforts to discharge employees who make inappropriate remarks. For example in the case of *Dowie v. Independent School District No. 141*, the court upheld the dismissal of a junior high school counselor who, among other things, repeatedly administered an oral survey to individuals and groups of junior high school students regarding their personal sexual activities; used vulgar, crude, and inappropriate language and stories when speaking to students; and breached the confidentiality of student whom he counseled, including disclosing an incest victims' confidences to teachers in a social setting.

The NASSP reports that in the case of *Penn-Delco School District v. Urso*, a dismissal upheld for a teacher who admitted to fantasies about spanking girls and who repeatedly threatened to spank a 17-year-old high school student, causing the student to become nervous and upset.

Sexual Harassment of Males

Although most victims of sexual harassment are girls, it must be acknowledged that boys are sometimes the victims of sexual harassment at school. According to Pat Mahony, boys are more likely to suffer sexual harassment if they do not conform to male stereotypes. Because of the apparent contempt that many boys hold for girls, boys emphasize their masculinity to prove that they are as unlike girls as possible. In fact, boys often use girls as their negative reference group. Mahony believes that in order to escape sexual harassment themselves, boys are pressured to adopt the sexual predatory behavior of their peers.

Mahony recounts a rather bizarre experiment conducted by a male teacher to determine whether his students were *normal.* In front of an all male class the teacher suddenly announced, "There's a naked woman running across the playground." All but one boy rushed to the window. As the boys were returning to their seats, the single boy who had remained seated objected to the experiment as sexist. The teacher announced to the class, "Now we know who isn't normal." Mahony reports that the teacher and class ridiculed the student and the other students physically abused him outside the classroom. Hopefully this is not an example of typical teacher or student behavior. However, it does indicate how being perceived as different and feminine can result in harassment.

In the AAUW study of sexual harassment in schools they reported that students would be very upset if they were called gay or lesbian. Being called gay would be more upsetting to boys than actual physical abuse. Interestingly, of those boys who have been called gay, more than half say they have called someone else gay.

Because sexual harassment is often a group activity, boys often feel pressure to go along with the harassment, in order to belong. The National School Safety Counsel argues, "In most cases, the identity of the victims is unimportant since the purpose of the activity is to prove masculinity. Many accounts of sexual harassment report strong peer support as evidenced by cheering and egging the offenders on." Clearly, policies must be written so that individuals are held accountable for their own actions.

Recent newspaper accounts have commented that sexist behavior by women may be a trend of the 1990s. While men have long been criticized for sexist actions and comments, women are gaining ground in that dubious arena. The Equal Employment Opportunity Commission has seen the number of sexual harassment complaints by men more that double in the past years. While it's still a fraction, roughly one-tenth, of those filed by women, more that 950 charges were filed by men in 1992, compared with 446 in 1989.

The *Manhattan Mercury* published a *Baltimore Sun* story that reported on the largest award ever for a male victim of sexual harassment. In 1993 a California court awarded Sabino Gutierrez $1 million in damages after a jury ruled that his female boss had sexually harassed him. He charged that he was subjected to unwanted caresses, fondling and demands for sex from his boss. In the same article, Susan Webb, is quoted as saying that "It's difficult for a woman to talk about harassment. But it's even more difficult for a man. He tends to get laughed out of the room. We have this underlying belief that men should be sexually available at all times, and like it."

Because men still have the best jobs and the most power, many women find it difficult to summon much sympathy for the idea that men are victims of sexual harassment. However, sexual harassment has serious consequences for all victims. A young male colleague told of the following incident that occurred to him during his first year as a high school teacher.

I knew very few people in the community. A female colleague in my department called and asked if I'd like to go have a beer and get acquainted. To be honest, I didn't remember meeting her, but I had met so many people so quickly that I didn't want to admit I didn't recall meeting her. I made polite excuses for several days, but she continued to call and invite me out. I eventually gave in so that she would not be offended and would stop calling.

I met her at a bar and she immediately moved her seat very close to mine. She probed me about my personal life and I did my best to answer her questions. Several of her friends arrived and she made me feel very uncomfortable. She told these other women to stay away because I was all hers. She told me that she had lots of materials for instruction that I could have but I would have to come over and get them. I decided to leave early. When I got home much later, my answering machine was full of messages from her. She had called eight times asking me to come over. It was after 2 AM.

In the weeks that followed, she left messages and sent me notes that were quite embarrassing. Each first year teacher was assigned an experienced teacher as a mentor. I turned to her and asked her what I should do. She told me this was an initiation that all new male teachers had been through. She laughed as did others who learned that I was the latest victim. They did not warn me assuming I was a "big boy" and could handle myself.

In a conversation with an administrator, I told about my uncomfortable welcome to the school. He commented that it was probably part of the territory for a "good-looking, young guy." He said that I should be flattered and not to worry about it. I am now comfortable and confident in my position, but I question whether it is fair for new teachers to face this dilemma. I was eager to be accepted and did not want people to think that I was making trouble. I wish I had handled this situation differently.

Some men and boys do not report sexual harassment because they think it is supposed to be real macho for a woman to grab their buns.   Others keep quiet because of peer pressure. Although men are just now starting to talk about it, it is likely that the topic of males being victims of sexual harassment will gain more attention, especially in light of the fact that Michael Crichton, author of *Jurassic Park*, has recently signed a contract for 3.5 million for the film rights to his yet unwritten novel about a man being sexually harassed by his female boss.

Although males who are victims of sexual harassment are in a similar situation to female victims, the fact that sexual harassment of females can lead to bodily harm makes the situations inherently different.

Sexual Harassment of Gay, Lesbian and Bisexual Students

Another type of discrimination is sexual harassment against gay, lesbian and bisexual students. These students face tremendous challenges as they grow up. According to the Center for Population Options; gay, lesbian and bisexual students face rejection, isolation, verbal harassment and physical violence in schools.

Although gender identity is established between the ages of 18 months and 5 years, most students come into awareness of their sexual orientation during adolescence. Although many gay, lesbian and bisexual students cope with the stress of adolescence with about the same degree of success as heterosexual students, a significant number are have difficulty coping. According to Joyce Hunter and Robert Schaecher nonacceptance of the adolescent's homosexuality can result in attempted or successful suicide. According to a 1989 study conducted by Paul Gibson for the U.S. Department of Health and Human Services, suicide is the leading cause of death among gay males, lesbian, bisexual and transsexual youth. Gay and lesbian students are two to three times more likely to attempt suicide than their heterosexual peers.

Although these students share the same basic needs for acceptance as other students, studies reported by the National Education Association (NEA) indicate gay and lesbian students are often at greater risk than other students for isolation, parental rejection, running away, and low self-esteem. According to the NEA homophobia and discrimination exist, in virtually all schools and often results in a lack of peer-group interaction, guidance by understanding role models, and instruction by sensitive educators. It appears that school counselors are not always helpful. A 1991 survey of secondary school counselors reported that one in six thought there were no gay students in their school, and 20 percent believed they were not very competent at counseling gay students.

According to the Center for Population Options, a 1986 study reported that 45 percent of the gay men and 20 percent of the lesbians surveyed were victims of verbal and physical assaults in secondary school because of their sexual orientation. Toleration of sexual harassment against gay and lesbian students often leads to ostracism and violence against these students. In its passive form this harassment results in a lack of protection for students from harassment and violence. In its more active form it exists as discrimination, open ridicule, treatment of homosexual students as mentally ill by teaching and guidance staffs, and violence.

The NEA recommends that all schools have policies that recognize the right of all students regardless of their sexual preference "to attend schools free of verbal and physical harassment; the right to attend schools where respect and dignity for all is standard; the right to have access to accurate information about themselves, free of negative judgment, and delivered by trained adults who not only inform them, but affirm them; the right to positive role models, both in person and the curriculum..."

Student-to-Teacher Sexual Harassment

As we conduct workshops and make presentations to students, teachers and administrators we are surprised by the number of teachers who asked us "is it possible for teachers to be sexually harassed by students?" As the teachers talked to us, it became clear that they knew that offensive behavior was taking place. What they wanted to know was, is this behavior sexual harassment?

Because of their age, education, maturity, experience, authority, and status it would seem that teachers have all of the power in the student-to-teacher relationship. However, teachers tell us that they have been embarrassed, degraded, undermined, and humiliated by students. Although not a scientific sample, we heard scores of stories of student-to-teacher sexual harassment. In most cases the victim was a female teacher.

One teacher told of a group of male athletes that would crowd around her desk at the end of class and close in around her as she tried to walk out of the room. Another teacher, who was single and lived alone, told us that she often received obscene phone calls late at night. Other teachers told of having male students comment on their bodies, sex lives, and what the students could do to satisfy the teacher's need for sex.

In a large group presentation a male administrator told the group, "It is impossible for a teacher to be sexually harassed by a student...A competent teacher should be able to handle this type of behavior." He went on to say, "If a teacher had good classroom control, this type of behavior would not happen." The heated discussion that his comments generated between members of the group, imply that student-to-teacher sexual harassment is not well understood. We asked the speaker what he would do if a female teacher was knocked to the ground and kicked in the hallway. He responded by saying that this was different. "This would be a case of assault and the students would be arrested." This exchange clearly demonstrates the tendency of men to blame the victim for her harassment. This administrator believed that it was some how the female teacher's fault that she was harassed. He believed that, either she did something to cause the harassment or she was not a good enough teacher to be able to prevent it.

Because many male high school students are physically larger than their female teachers they may be physically intimidating to many of their female teachers. This physical intimidation is a significant factor in student-to-teacher sexual harassment.

We are unaware of any studies that have examined student-to-teacher sexual harassment in public schools. However, Grauerholz conducted a study of this type of harassment by asking women college faculty members about behaviors directed toward them by students. He wanted to find out what behaviors occurred, whether the faculty members saw these behaviors as sexual harassment, and whether the professor had taken any actions to eliminate the behaviors. He found that the behaviors ranged from mild to severe, and there was a strong agreement that these behaviors constituted sexual harassment.

Sexist comments by male students toward female professors ranked as the most frequent form of sexual harassment.

Approximately one in three faculty members indicated that they experienced this form of harassment. Other forms of harassment included: undue attention (18 percent), obscene phone calls (17 percent), verbal sexual comments (15 percent), body language (12 percent), written comments (8 percent), sexual propositions (3 percent), physical advances (2 percent), sexual bribery (1percent), and sexual assault (.5 percent). Almost two-thirds of the victims of this form of sexual harassment reported that they did nothing, and only three percent filed a formal complaint with the university.

The following incidents were reported by two middle school administrators. Both incidents occurred before to the administrators had received any training regarding sexual harassment. The following incident occurred while the principal was supervising lunch period.

> I was supervising lunch period when I noticed a great deal of commotion at one of the tables. The boys and girls were whooping, laughing and shouting back and forth to one another. As I approached the table a seventh grade girl stared at me, grasped the banana she was holding in both hands, took it into her mouth and started to move her head up and down. As I reached the table, she continued to look at me and started to lick the banana in a "suggestive" manner.
>
> I asked her to quit doing what she was doing. Later I discussed the situation with the girl's mother. The mother did not believe that her daughter did what I described. I dropped that matter and made a mental note not to be alone with this student.

Another middle school principal reported that he was in his office when a seventh grade male student arrived with a note from the female band instructor.

The note informed me that the boy was sent to my office because he had been simulating a sex act in front to the band instructor and several female band members. The note reported that the band instructor had observed the young man holding his throat and rubbing it up and down emulating masturbation. Apparently the boy accompanied this action by oozing spit out from between is lips. This boy had previously been counseled for telling sex-based jokes to unwilling female students.

I told the boy that what he had done could be construed as sexual innuendo and that it was inappropriate behavior. The boy was given a day of in-school suspension.

Group Harassment

The most obscene and disgusting forms of sexual harassment involve groups of harassers. In 1993 the headlines were filled with stories of group harassment. In Los Angeles young men who called themselves the Posse competed for points for sexual conquests. Members of this group admitted to raping and molesting girls as young as 10 years old. In Glen Ridge, New Jersey 12 teenage boys gathered in a friend's basement to watch sexual acts performed on a mentally retarded 17 year old girl. The girl was sexually violated with a baseball bat, a stick, and a broom handle.

In *Peer Harassment: Hassles for Women on Campus*, O'Gorman Hughes and Sandler report that "men often do things in groups that they would not do alone....Whatever the reasons, when men are in a group they may say or do hostile things to women that they might not otherwise do as individuals....When men outnumber women...incidents of harassment are more likely to occur."

Several of the following examples of group harassment are adapted from Jean O'Gorman Hughes and Bernice Sandler's *Peer Harassment* .

√   "Scoping," describing and rating women's attractiveness on a scale of one to ten. This frequently occurs in libraries, study halls, cafeterias or other places where women pass by a group of men. This rating usually is accompanied by loud discussion of the woman's rating and her sexual attributes.

√   "Mooning," whereby men pull down their pants and show their buttocks aggressively. This is usually done by a group of men to one or more women.

√   "Sharking," whereby one male breaks away from a group of his friends and bites a woman on her breast.

√   "Spiking," whereby one or more males pull down the pants of a female.

√   "Flipping," whereby one or more males lift a girl's skirt up over her waist.

√   "Flashing," whereby one or more males expose their genitals to a single girl or group of girls.

Harassment by Non-Employees

It must be remembered that schools have an obligation to prevent sexual harassment in the school by *anyone*, including harassers who are not employed by the school district. Although we are not aware of any school-based court cases that have addressed this issue, we interpret the EEOC guidelines to mean that school districts are responsible for acts of sexual harassment by non-employees if the school administration knew or should have known of the conduct and failed to take immediate corrective action. The school is accountable for the actions of anyone who is in the school by invitation or with the permission of the school district. Consequently school districts should make sure that their notice against sexual harassment is prominently displayed.

Responsibility of School Employees to Supervise

Because students are compelled by state laws to attend school, they are not there by their own choice. Therefore, school children are protected by the Eighth Amendment of the U.S. Constitution, against state actions that constitute cruel and unusual punishment. States are increasingly holding school districts responsible for maintaining safe schools, in the belief that forcing children to attend crime-infested schools constitutes cruel and unusual punishment. California lead the nation in this area when it amended it's constitution to include the mandatory provision: "Right to Safe Schools." All students and staff of primary, elementary, middle/junior high and senior high schools have the inalienable right to attend campuses which are safe, secure and peaceful.

According to the National School Safety Center, "This amendment was passed because it was believed that school children are twice-victimized; (1) when they become actual victims of school-related crime, violence, disruption, or fear; and (2) when they are thereby denied their rights to a quality education in a tranquil learning environment."

Because courts commonly hold teachers and school districts liable for negligence, some courts are beginning to extend this accountability to protection from sexual harassment. If school administrators have previous knowledge of incidents of sexual harassment, they have an obligation to warn and protect potential victims. By the same token, if they know of previous violent or antisocial activities of a particular student, they need to take steps to prevent further violence.

Legal Protection Against Sex Discrimination

For the past twenty years legislators at the state and federal levels have been grappling with the issues surrounding sex discrimination. This struggle has resulted in laws being passed that set forth standards and procedures for ensuring nondiscrimination. The goal of all of these enactments is to ensure nondiscrimination and educational equity for both males and females. Sex discrimination in schools is prohibited by the following federal laws. The statutes, regulations and other legal sources mentioned below may be obtained from a law library, by contacting the agency responsible for enforcement, or a member of Congress.

Title VII of the Civil Rights Act of 1964 as amended by the Equal Employment Opportunity Act of 1972, the Pregnancy Discrimination Act of 1978 and the Civil Rights Act of 1991 prohibits employers employing more than 15 individuals from discriminating on the basis of race, color, religion, sex or national origin in all aspects of employment. The 1972 amendments permit employees and applicants to file suit in federal district court if they are not satisfied with the employers disposition of their complaints. This act covers all aspects of employment including pay, promotion, hiring, dismissal and working conditions. As amended in 1991, it allows sexual harassment plaintiffs to sue for monetary damages, allows recovery of compensatory damages only in cases of intentional discrimination and punitive damages only against non-public employers who act with malice or reckless indifference. The damages are currently capped depending on the number of employees.

In the fall of 1993 the U.S. Supreme Court is expected to hear arguments on a non-school sexual harassment case that could have significant implications for schools. The case of *Harris v. Forklift Systems* raises the question of whether employees alleging sexual harassment on the job must prove psychological injury in order to collect damages under Title VII. The Sixth Circuit Court of Appeals dismissed the case even after the plaintiff had shown that her boss subjected her to "a continuing pattern of sex-based derogatory conduct." The Court said she was unable to prove that the abuse affected her "psychological well-being." Two federal courts of appeal have agreed with the Sixth Circuit, but two others have held that plaintiffs need only prove the existence of a "hostile work environment" to be able to recover damages.

Women's Educational Equity Act of 1974 promotes educational equity for women through a program of discretionary grants and contracts. The act was reauthorized and substantially revised by the Education Amendments of 1978.

The **Carl D. Perkins Vocational Education Act of 1984** is a comprehensive effort to infuse sex equity into educational programs. This act requires positive action to end bias and stereotyping as well as to ensure nondiscrimination. It requires that each state hire at least one full-time staff person to coordinate and infuse sex equity throughout the vocational education system.

Executive Order 11246 as amended by Executive Order 11375 as amended by Executive Order 12086 prohibits employment discrimination in federal contracts. All federal contracts must contain a nondiscrimination clause in which the contractor agrees not to discriminate in any aspect of employment.

Title IX of the Education Amendments of 1972 prohibits discrimination on the basis of sex in educational programs or activities which receive federal financial assistance. Title IX covers both employees and students and virtually all activities of a school district. The prohibition covers discrimination in employment of teachers and other school personnel as well as discrimination in admissions, financial aid, and access to educational programs and activities. Title IX states: *"No person in the United States shall on the basis of sex be excluded from participating in, be denied the benefits of or be subjected to discrimination under any education program or activity receiving federal financial assistance."* In general, Title IX is enforced by the Department of Education. Under Title IX students may sue to collect monetary damages from the school or the school may lose federal funds.

State Laws. Every state has some form of gender discrimination law. As we mentioned earlier, the amount of attention that state legislatures have given to the issue of sexual harassment varies from state to state. To find out the applicable law in your state contact your state Civil Rights Commission located in the state capital.

When we make presentations on the legal rights of victims of sexual harassment and other forms of sex discrimination, we are frequently asked the following questions: Who can sue? How do you file a complaint? How long do I have to file a complaint? Who can make a complaint? How quickly must the investigation be completed? And, what are the punishments allowed? The following chart answers these questions.

Answers to Questions About
Federal Avenues for Redress

Entitlement	Who Can Sue	How Do I File	When Must I Act	Time For Investigation	Punishment Allowed
14th Amendment U.S. Constitution	Employees and students	Varies	Varies from state to state	Varies	Compensatory and punitive damages, and injunctive relief
Title VII	Employees and applicants	Complaints are called "charges" and can be in person, by letter or by EEOC form.	180 days to file charges with EEOC 90 days to sue in court.	120 days to complete investigation, "so far as practicable."	Courts may order behavior stopped and award relief, including back pay.
Title IX	Employees and students	By letter or complaint form obtained from Department of Education	180 days unless unless extended "for good cause"	Statute requires "prompt investigation."	Compensatory damages and injunctive relief.
Civil Rights Act of 1991	Employees and students	By letter or complaint form obtained from Department of Educaiton	180 days unless unless extended "for good cause"	Statute requires "prompt investigation."	Compensatory damages and injunctive relief.

Proposed Federal Legislation

The growing national awareness of the way that girls are being shortchanged in our nations schools has resulted in the introduction of an omnibus legislative package. Anne Bryant, Executive Director of the American Association of University Women, calls this legislation "real progress toward providing America's girls with an educational environment that is equitable and free from bias." In April of 1993, The Gender Equity Education Act was introduced by Representatives Schroeder, Snowe, and Kildee. The package addresses the important areas of education reform related to gender equity including: teacher training; teen pregnancy and drop-out prevention; the establishment of an Office of Gender Equity in the Department of Education; funding for gender-fair teaching practices in math and science; the expansion of the Women's Educational Equity Act which promotes the use of gender equity programs and materials, and incentives to eliminate sexual harassment and abuse in schools. If approved, this act will amend the Elementary and Secondary Education Act of 1965.

Included in this package is H.B. 1795, The Sexual Harassment Free Schools Act. Representative Olympia Snowe introduced this bill for the purpose of authorizing a research and development front and an implementation grant for programs to address sexual harassment and violence. It would also expand the definition of an "effective schools program" to include an environment free from sexual harassment and abuse and would authorize funds under the Programs for the Improvement of Comprehensive School Health Education to be used for sexual harassment and assault programs.

Examples of Sexual Harassment

The following is a representative list of behaviors that a court might likely find to be sexual harassment.

√   A male teacher or student continually makes sexually explicit comments to a female student.

√   A male teacher propositions a female student.

√   A male teacher or student subjects female students to obscene pictures, unwanted touching and/or verbal sexual abuse.

√   A female student is depicted in sexually explicit cartoons or comments written on the boys' rest room walls.

√   A male teacher touches a female student repeatedly, makes suggestive comments, or asks her to have sex with him.

√   A group of male students stand in the halls and make sexual comments and proposition female students as they pass by.

√   Male teachers or students forcibly grab, hug, or kiss female students.

√   Male teachers or students flip up female students' dresses, pull down their pants, or grab their bodies.

√   Repeated and persistent requests for a date in the face of a clear indication of a lack of interest.

Examples Non-Sexual Harassment

√   A male teacher or student on one occasion pressed against a female student as they passed in the hallway.

√   A pin-up type photo is posted in the metal shop area, that is promptly removed at the order of the principal.

√   An isolated example of gender-related jokes or sexual teasing.

√   A single unwelcome request for a date.

Defenses Against Charges of Sexual Harassment

Just as students have a right to be free from incidents of sexual harassment, teachers and students have a right to be free from false charges of sexual harassment. The school district's policy against sexual harassment should include a prohibition against making a false claim. And there should be significant punishments for making false complaints of sexual harassment.

As we stated earlier, even in valid cases of sexual harassment, students seldom report the alleged misconduct to the alleged harasser. Consequently a teacher or student who is accused of sexual harassment often does not learn of the charge until a formal complaint has been filed.

The alleged victim will typically tell a friend, parent or other school employee that the alleged harasser committed some specific act which the victim believes was sexual harassment. Even if the report is accurate the harasser is often caught off guard. Villaume and Foley report that the accused person usually feels abandoned, lonely, violated, and lost amidst the legal proceedings. They feel like they are out of control of their lives and their careers.

Villaume and Folley believe that educators should know what an investigation will be like so that they are prepared to respond appropriately if they are ever accused of sexual harassment. As we stated earlier, a charge of sexual harassment can end a career and cost a person incredible emotional and financial damage. This is particularly true if the charges include grounds for criminal action or discharge from employment. It is typical for an accused teacher to be suspended with pay until the investigation is completed.

Although a teacher has a right to make a statement, Villaume and Foley recommend that the teacher not make any statement and immediately contact their teacher organization for legal representation. If the teacher is not a member of a teacher organization, they should contact a lawyer directly.

If a charge of sexual harassment is not able to be resolved within the school district and proceeds to the courts, there are some defenses that seem to be accepted and some that are rejected. According to the Utah Department of Human Resource Management, examples of defenses that may be allowed in sexual harassment cases include:

√   No harassment occurred.

√   Any advances were not unwelcome. They were solicited, incited or encouraged.

√   Harassment was not based upon sex, overtures were made to both sexes or conduct was equally offensive to both sexes.

√   Employer had legitimate non-discriminatory reasons for the conduct.

√   Harassment was not sufficiently severe or pervasive to alter the conditions of employment and create an abusive environment.

√   Employer had no knowledge of the harassment and there was a grievance avenue for claims.

√   Employer, with knowledge, took prompt and remedial action.

Examples of defenses that would probably not be considered in sexual harassment cases include:

√   The claimant's failure to verbalize disapproval of the sexually harassing behavior is not a protection for the behavior.

√   Whether or not the complainant participated voluntarily in the harassing behavior cannot be used as a defense for the accused.

√   Although a "sexually provocative" behavior, speech, dress and or demeanor may be admissible in a sexual harassment proceeding, it is not a defense for inappropriate behavior by the harasser.

Chapter Five

Framework For Practice

When a student brings a charge of sexual harassment or reports an activity that appears to be a case of sexual harassment, the school should have a specific procedure to follow. Ideally, each school building should have a person trained and available so that students have someone to go to for advice without having to make a formal complaint. In this chapter we will present a description of the investigation process.

How Should Students Deal With Sexual Harassment?

Ignoring sexual harassment will not end it. Forty-six percent of the victims of harassment try this strategy, but only one of four succeed in getting the harasser to stop. Schools need to teach students how to deal with sexual harassment. The successful of the following suggestions will be partially determined by the age of the student. Obviously, most junior high or senior high students will be better able to follow through with these suggestions, while a first grade student will need more adult assistance. The following chart depicts how a student should respond to an incident of sexual harassment.

Sexual Harassment:
How You Should Respond

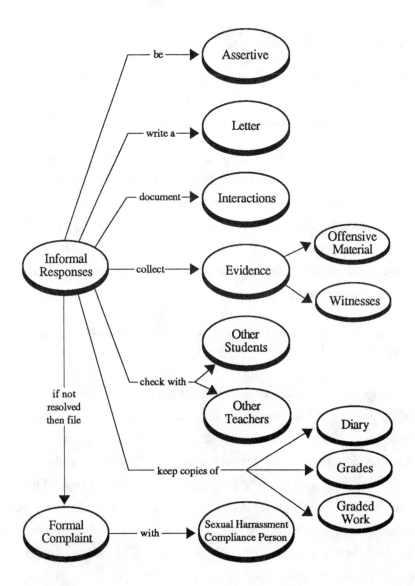

Teacher's And Parent's Roles

√   **Teach your students to be assertive.** It is difficult for an adult to be assertive with a harasser, so make sure you role play with your students. Role playing will help them deal with the situation and give them appropriate words to say. Tell them not to apologize, they are being harassed--not the other way around. Students need to understand that it is all right to be honest and direct. They need to be able to say that they find a certain behavior offensive.

√   **Tell your students to report the behavior to an adult.** No child should feel threatened, intimidated, or frightened. School should be a safe place that is conducive to learning. Children will not be able to learn if they don't feel safe. Children can report the behavior to a teacher, counselor, or principal. If your school has a specific policy for sexual harassment, make sure that all students know to whom they should report incidents of sexual harassment.

√   **If your students are frightened to talk to an adult at school,** parents should be encouraged to report the behavior to the teacher and principal.

√   **Encourage parents to document** their children's encounters with sexual harassment. They should note the frequency of the harassment and the date, time, and place of each occurrence. They should include the names of everyone involved particularly if the child can name any witnesses to the harassment. Documentation should be as contemporaneous with the event as possible. The

EEOC and many courts have strongly supported the value of a contemporaneous complaint or protest. Documentation should describe the harasser's words and behavior as well what as the child said and how the behavior made the child feel.

√   **Teachers and parents should check with other parents.** Don't assume that this is happening only to one child. Ask parents if their child will verify what happened or if their child is having similar problems. If another child has witnessed an incident, ask the parents if their child is willing to verify what happened.

√   **File a formal complaint.** If, after the incident is reported to school officials, the behavior continues, file a formal complaint. Follow the procedures outlined by the school district in their sexual harassment policy. After all avenues have been exhausted file a formal complaint with the EEOC. IMPORTANT: You have only 180 days from the occurrence to file a formal complaint.

Unfortunately children don't like their parents to complain to school officials. They often endure sexual harassment because they feel like teachers and students will retaliate or they will be considered "troublemakers". Teachers who are experiencing sexual harassment have these same fears. Many think they have to put up with sexual harassment or quit their jobs. They fear if they report the behavior it will result in a lower grade or some other form of punishment. Sexual harassment is illegal. They need to be reminded that just as sexual harassment is illegal, retaliation is, too.

Talking With School Personnel About Sexual Harassment

It is important to remember that many parents do not feel comfortable in schools, and even those who do may find it difficult to talk about behavior of a sexual nature. Educators must help parents learn about their rights and the rights of their children. They must be reminded that most educators are kind, compassionate people who want the best for their students.

However, parents must also realize that no educator can see everything that happens when there are 25-30 children in their classrooms. They can't see or hear everything that occurs on the playground when they supervise 50-80 children. A bus driver concerned with getting your child to school safely won't always be aware of everything that happens on the bus.

Parents should be encouraged to approach school personnel knowing that they want to help and are concerned about every child. Arm them with the following pointers:

√ **Keep calm and don't become defensive.** Tell the principal or teacher that you are concerned about your son/daughter and need help to solve the problem. State the problem and give as many details as possible (witnesses to the behavior, time, date, place any information that will help in the investigation.)

√ **Ask how the problem will be handled.** You need to know when the principal or teacher will get back to you and how the matter will be investigated. If you want things kept confidential, ask how this request will impede the process. Most of the time if you want the harassment stopped, all parties involved will have to know who, what, when, where, and how everything happened.

√   **Ask the principal or teacher if the school has a sexual harassment policy.** You will need to know if the problem will be dealt with as sexual harassment or a routine disciplinary matter. If the school does not have a policy on sexual harassment, share the sample policies in this book and suggest that they develop one. You might even volunteer to serve on a school improvement committee to develop a sexual harassment policy.

√   **Continue to go back to the principal or teacher if the behavior does not stop.** Proceed through the chain of command and exhaust all possibilities before filing a complaint with the EEOC.

Conducting An Investigation

Each school building should have a person designated to oversee any complaints of sexual harassment. This person can be the principal, assistant principal, counselor or teacher. We recommend that at each school consider ensuring that one male and one female are trained as investigators so that he investigator will be the same sex as the alleged victim. This person should ensure that all faculty and staff are trained to identify and eradicate sexual harassment. The sexual harassment policy should be prominently displayed in the school, printed in the student and teacher handbooks, and distributed to all parents.

All students, parents, and teachers should attend an orientation in which the policy and the consequences of sexual harassment are clearly explained. All students should learn how to file a formal complaint of sexual harassment. It is very important that the investigation procedures used are fair to all parties and do not further the victimization of the person making the claim of sexual harassment.

If a formal complaint is made, or if the sexual harassment compliance person believes that there is a probability that sexual harassment has occurred, he or she should talk with the person that the student first contacted to get an overall picture of the situation.

Interview With Complainant

Once a formal complaint is filed, the compliance person should meet with the complainant to find out what happened and what the student complainant wants done. The compliance person should remain calm and work to make the interviewing atmosphere as relaxed as possible. He or she should start the meeting by assuring the student that the details of the complaint will remain as confidential as is prudent. Webb suggests that the compliance person should (1) avoid expressing opinions, (2) avoid taking sides, (3) develop the list of questions before the interview process starts, and (4) remember to ask the same questions of all parties involved.

The compliance person should gather specific details about the incident. Generalities or openings such as "He flirted with me," "He's sexist," or "You know what he's like" are not acceptable. Open-ended questions better serve the rights of the victim and the accused. Questions should be phrased as requests to allow the student to give more than a "yes" or "no" answer (i.e., "Please tell me about the incident." or "Give me some examples of the behavior you found offensive.") To ensure that complete and accurate information is gathered, the questioner might ask the following:

1. Describe the offensive behavior.

2. Where did it take place?

3. When did it take place?

4. How many times did it occur?

5. Describe your feelings at the time the harassment occurred.

6. What was your response at the time the harassment occurred?

7. Did you tell anyone about the incident after it occurred?

8. Whom did you tell? When and what did you tell that person?

9. What was that person's response?

10. Describe any incidents of retaliation.

11. Show me any documentation that you have of the offensive behavior. (Journals, pictures, cartoons, jokes, etc.)

The compliance person should attempt to determine how the offensive behavior affected the complainant. Did it precipitate embarrassment, physical illness, a need for psychological counseling, trouble with schoolwork? The compliance person should press for details if necessary.

The complainant should be asked what he or she wants done to solve the problem. Possible solutions include a cessation of the offensive behavior, an apology, a transfer out of a class or activity where the harassment occurs, counseling for the victim and/or the harasser, or punishment of the harasser. Punishment, if the harasser is a teacher, could range from a reprimand to termination and criminal charges. If the harasser is a student, punishment could range from a reprimand to expulsion and criminal charges.

The compliance person should work with the complainant to make a list of possible witnesses. The list should increase until the compliance person is certain that he or she can glean enough information to make an informed decision about the matter. The list should include the names of those who have been told of the offensive behavior, and those who may have experienced being victims of similar offensive behavior. (It is better to collect too much data than to collect too little).

The complainant should be reassured that the district will not tolerate retaliation for making a complaint and that he or she should report any perceived retaliation immediately. The complainant may also have to be told that a full-scale investigation will be launched.

The compliance person should write a report about the interview meeting and have the complainant check it for accuracy. The complainant's parents should be informed about the outcome of this initial meeting. And, the compliance person may choose to share the report with the school district's attorney.

The Investigation

When an investigation is initiated, the original compliance person becomes the investigator. It is wise, at this point, to revisit the witness list with the complainant to ensure that it is complete. The investigator then faces the monumental decision of whom to interview first. If witnesses or other victims are not involved, or if the problem can be solved between the harasser and the victim, the obvious choice is to talk to the accused first. But if there are other victims, or it the complainant is afraid of the harasser, or if the harasser may become defensive, it may be best to interview the harasser last.

During the interviews, detailed notes should be taken. Key phrases should be written down so that details can be filled in after the interview. Webb suggests that because not every word needs to be written exactly, it is not necessary that a tape recorder be used.

After the interviews are completed, the investigator should examine the notes for common threads and make a determination about what happened. The EEOC guidelines and the local school district policy should include helpful criteria for determining whether or not sexual harassment has occurred. Many times the situation will not be totally clear, but a decision and a recommendation must be made anyway. The findings in the case should be made available only to those with a valid reason to be informed of them.

The investigator should attempt to determine how the offensive behavior affected the complainant? What did the complainant do as a result of the harassment? (e.g. anger, embarrassment, physical illness, psychological counseling, trouble doing schoolwork, etc.) Determine if the complainant objected to the behavior or comments or indicate it was unwelcome? If so, how? What was the response of the harasser? Was there any retaliation by the alleged harasser? If so, what was it? You may need to press for details.

At this point we suggest that you ask the complainant what he or she wants done to solve this problem. Find out if they want the behavior stopped, an apology, transfer from the class or activity, counseling for the victim, or punishment of the harasser. If the harasser is a teacher the punishment could range from a reprimand, to termination and criminal charges. If the harasser is a student the punishment could range from a reprimand to expulsion and criminal charges. Once you have collected the details you should summarize the complaints and allow the complainant to confirm the report's accuracy.

This is a complex issue because, at this point, you have to consider the interest of the student as well as the school district. If the student says that she just wanted to talk to someone and does not want anything done, the school district may be exposed to later liability if a future law suite is filed and it is determined that the school knew of the offensive behavior and did nothing. Although consideration should be given to honoring the wishes of the complainant, we reluctantly recommend that all complaints be followed up with a documented investigation.

At this point the investigator should obtain the names of all other persons who may have witnessed the offensive behavior. The investigator should also get the names of any other people that have been told of the offensive behavior. If possible obtain the names of any other persons who the complainant believes may have also been victims of similar behavior.

The meeting with the complainant should conclude by assuring the student that the district will not tolerate retaliation for making a complaint. The student should be told to report any retaliation immediately. The complainant should be told that an investigation will be conducted and he or she will be informed of the outcome. At this point the investigator may wish to share this report with the school district's attorney.

After a complaint is filed, the compliance person becomes the investigator. At this point, the investigator should decide who will be interviewed next, the harasser, other witnesses, or other victims. The investigator will have to decide this from initial information gathered from the student and/or teacher. If witnesses or other victims are not involved, or if the problem can be resolved between the harasser and the victim, the obvious choice is to talk to the person accused of the harassment. But if there are other victims, or if the student is afraid of the harasser, or if the harasser will become defensive, it may be best to interview the alleged harasser last.

Sample Questions to Ask Witnesses:

1. One of your students (fellow students) has complained about some behaviors of (name alleged harasser.) Tell me what you know about the situation. (If the person describes harassment, the same questions may be asked as were asked of the complainant. If the person doesn't know anything, the next two questions might be asked.)

2. Have you ever had a problem with either person?

3. Do you know anybody who can clarify the situation?

Interview of Alleged Harasser

Indicate to the alleged harasser that the school district has a policy prohibiting sexual harassment, that there has been a complaint against him or her, and that it is the investigator's job to determine whether there is a problem and, if so, to resolve it appropriately. The complainant, the behavior in question, and its effects should be identified. Ask these questions:

Questions to Ask Alleged Harasser:

1. One of your students (fellow students), (name student), has complained about some of your behaviors at school. Can you tell me more about the situation? What happened? What did you do or say?

2. (Describe some of the behaviors reported by the named student.) Can you tell me anything that will clarify the situation? What did you intend? Why did you do this?

3. Did the complainant object or complain? If so how? Did the complainant seem upset? Did the complainant say or do anything to make you think behavior was welcome? What did you do or say?

4. If the alleged harasser denies that the incident took place. As: Do you consider the complainant to be a liar and, if so, why do you think the complainant is lying? Have you ever had a problem with the complainant.

5. Confront the alleged harasser with the reports of any witnesses. Ask the alleged harasser to comment or explain these reports.

Remind the alleged harasser that the sexual harassment policy encourages students to complain; that there can be no retaliation for making a complaint and that the alleged harasser should take no action which could be viewed as retaliatory regardless of the alleged harasser's opinion of the validity of the complaint. Determine if the alleged harasser knows of any witnesses that he or she can offer to rebut the allegations. Inform the alleged harasser that the claim will be investigated fully and with the greatest degree of confidentiality possible.

How Should A Student Confront A Harasser?

We must let our children know that confronting a student or teacher harasser is not an easy thing to do. However, we must also let them know that they have a right to be free from harassment and have a right to see that sexual harassment is stopped. Students who experience sexual harassment want it to stop; want to go to school in an safe nonthreatening atmosphere. Students should be told that they must assess the situation and determine whether the behavior is unwanted. If it is, then they should take action to stop it.

As we said earlier, it is common for a victim of sexual harassment to try to ignore the offensive behavior. In a recent study that we conducted, we found that the most frequent response to sexual harassment was to "discuss it with a friend." Only 19 percent told the principal and only eighteen percent told their parents.

According to Sandroff, approximately one-third of the harassers who were told to stop did so. If the victim ignores sexual harassment the harasser can argue that he thought the activity was welcomed. It is imperative that victims of sexual harassment make it clear to the harasser that they consider his behavior inappropriate and expect it to stop. Because sexual harassment is a matter of perception, the victim's perception of the behavior must be made visible if she wants to avoid further harassment. The harasser must be put on notice that the line has been crossed, the behavior is offensive, and that it will not be tolerated.

Students who are victims of sexual harassment should take the following steps when confronting the harasser.

√   **Be assertive**. Be honest and direct. Say you find the behavior offensive. Don't apologize ("I'm sorry, but I didn't like..."). You are the one being harassed, not the other way around. Don't hint or be evasive ("I'm busy tonight" or "I have other plans"). So say "no" clearly ("The answer is no. Don't ask again." Or, "I've told you before that I'm not interested in that kind of relationship, so stop asking me.") Some men still claim that women mean yes when they don't specifically say no. Body language is important when confronting a harasser. Your tone of voice should be even and firm, make eye contact, be aware of your posture (don't hunch or fold your arms in front of you), and be as confident as possible. If you are nervous about confronting your harasser, rehearse what you will say with a friend.

√   **Write the harasser a letter.** While some people may be able to be assertive, others may not feel comfortable speaking directly to a harasser. For these people, a letter is an excellent confrontational tool. The concept of writing a letter was originated by Mary Rowe and further developed by Bernice Sandler. Sandler reminds us that "the letter should be polite, low key, and detailed." It should consist of a factual account of the incident complete with a description of how the writer feels about the event and an explanation of what the writer wants to happen next. If the writer believes the harassment will continue or escalate, he or she must tell the harasser what action will be taken to get it to stop. The writer should be direct or the letter will be ineffective in helping to accomplish the desired goal. To assure that the letter conveys the writer's intent clearly, a second opinion may be requested from a trusted individual. A copy of the school district's sexual harassment policy may be attached to the letter.

A copy of the letter should be kept; it will serve as valuable evidence later that the writer's communication was clear about his or her wishes. Sandler suggests that the letter be delivered in person or by registered or certified mail.

Above all, the writer must do what he or she says in the letter will happen. Idle threats should not be made. (See Appendix A for a sample letter).

√   **Document the incidents.** Keep a journal. Note the date(s), time(s), and place(s) that the harassment occurred. It is important to describe the event in as much detail as you can. Describe the harasser's words and behavior. Write down what you said, what you did, and how you felt. Document how the harassment is affecting your school performance or health. Include the names of everyone involved, particularly if you have witnesses that can verify what happened. Your documentation should be as contemporaneous with the incident as possible. The EEOC and many courts have strongly supported the value of contemporaneous complaints or protests.

√   **Collect evidence.** Do whatever you can to collect the evidence that your school operates with a hostile educational environment. If there are sexual cartoons or jokes posted on the bulletin board confiscate them. William Petrocelli and Barbara Repa recommend that if you can't remove the offensive items, make a copy or take a photograph of the material. If you are a girl and the offensive material is in the boys rest room, have a male friend copy the exact language for you. If you are unable or unwilling to remove or reproduce the offensive material, you should make a written description of it in as much detail as possible.

√   **Check with other students.** You should assume there is no such thing as a first-time sexual harasser. Ask your friends if something similar has happened to them. A complaint backed up by others makes retaliation less likely and gives support to your complaint.

√   **Keep copies of your grades and graded work.** If the harasser is a teacher, you should be able to document any adverse grade or treatment that has occurred as a result of your refusal to accept his behavior.

√   **File a formal complaint.** If the sexual harassment continues, you should make a formal complaint. Students do not always make formal complaints for a variety of reasons. Some do not understand that they have a right to be free from sexual harassment at school. Some do not want to risk losing the acceptance of their peers. Some fear that they will be the one being punished. Some fear retaliation. Although it is sometimes hard to take formal action, sexual harassment will likely get worse if unreported. Sandler offers a word of caution: Because any action you take may provoke a reaction, be sure of what you are going to say and what you want to happen.

What Educators Can Do

Some people believe that the only way to stop sexual harassment is through legislative action and law suits. However, we believe that there are at least five distinct steps that educators can take in order to eradicate sexual harassment our schools.

First, everyone must recognize that sexual harassment is a serious problem. It is hard for many educators to acknowledge that school is not the place it once was. It is comforting to believe that when children enter school they will be safe and all of their experiences will be positive. The existence of sexual harassment must be affirmed before it can be stopped.

Second, educators, parents, and students need to understand and analyze the causes of sexual harassment before productive action can be taken.. Third the feeling of outrage is necessary in order for us to do more than just wish our schools were free of sexual harassment. Fourth, we must talk to children and their parents, and explain the serious consequences of sexual harassment. They must see the connection between sexual stereotyping, sexism, and sexual harassment. And finally, our school districts must develop a comprehensive policy prohibiting all forms of sexual harassment, train all staff and students, and then monitor behavior to ensure that sexual harassment is not taking place.

What Students Can Do

Most victims of sexual harassment use informal remedies to resolve it. If a student believes that the person who is harassing her does not know that the behavior is offensive, simply telling him to stop will often makes things better. Threatening to tell a teacher, a counselor, or your parent (and doing it if necessary)is also an effective action. If the offensive behavior continues the student may wish to file an official grievance through your school's grievance procedure. If you are still being bothered you can file a discrimination complaint or contact an attorney and file a lawsuit.

Students should be certain that their school has a policy prohibiting sexual harassment and that every teacher and student is aware of the policy.

If you even suspect that something is not right or that you are being sexually harassed, you should immediately tell your parents about the offensive behavior. It is very helpful if you write down the date, times, and your best memory of what was said or done to you during the harassment. If the harassment persists, inform a trusted teacher, counselor, or administrator. Report any efforts at retaliation, reduction of grade, loss of privilege, or threats by the harasser or his friends.

If the victim believes that his or her school is not adequately responding to the complaints a formal sexual harassment grievance may be filed. If the outcome is not satisfactory, the student may contact the state Office for Civil Rights, the U.S. Department of Education Office of Civil Rights or obtain the services of an attorney.

What Victims of Sexual Harassment Should Not Do

O'Gorman Hughes and Sandler advise that there are three things that victims of sexual harassment should avoid:

√ **Don't blame yourself.** Sexual harassment is not something that a woman brings on herself; it is action that the harasser decides to take. It is not your fault. Blaming yourself only turns your anger inward and can lead to depression. You need to turn your anger outward, against the appropriate person, the harasser.

√ **Don't delay**. If you delay action when someone harasses you, it is likely to continue. Also, if you delay filing charges, you may find out that you have missed the time limit for doing so.

√ **Don't keep it to yourself.** By being quiet about sexual harassment, you enable it to continue. Chances are extremely good that you are not the only victim. Speaking up can protect other people from also becoming victims. Additionally, not telling anyone encourages feelings of helplessness which can lead to self-blame and, ultimately, depression.

Chapter Six

Successful Programs of Sexual Harassment Prevention

We believe that educators can make significant progress toward eradicating sexual harassment from our schools. We've seen evidence that change of the nature required to solve the problem of sexual harassment is possible. According to *How Schools Shortchange Girls,* "A review of research on how books influence children cited 23 studies that demonstrated that books do transmit values to young readers, that multi-cultural readings produce markedly more favorable attitudes toward non-dominant groups than do all-white curricula, that academic achievement for all students was positively correlated with use of nonsexist and multi-cultural materials, and that sex-role stereotyping was reduced in those student whose curriculum portrayed females and males in non-stereotypical roles."

Change is possible! Sexism, gender bias and sexual harassment can be eradicated. Certainly, it requires effort, but it can be done. As a result of commitment, effort, and education some school districts have developed programs that are changing the way that boys and girls relate to one another.

As we have documented and discussed the trauma of sexual harassment and the failings of many schools to protect our children, we have not meant to imply that educators are universally ignoring the problem. Such is not the case. In fact, there are many examples where tremendous effort has been exerted and significant progress is being made in the fight for gender equity and humane communication across sex lines.

Many teachers, parents, and administrators are dealing with the hard questions and difficult issues surrounding sexual harassment. We applaud their efforts and urge them to continue. In the pages that follow, we have presented examples of programs that we found to be particularly noteworthy.

A District Wide Program to Eradicate Sexual Harassment

South Washington County Schools in Cottage Grove, Minnesota is one example of the many school districts that have a long history of working to eradicate sexual harassment. They first adopted their policy prohibiting sexual harassment and sexual violence in 1986. The policy was amended to its present form in 1990. This school district takes sexual harassment very seriously and has done a number of things to implement the policy.

According to Perry Palin, Human Resources Manager for the district, the most important factor in contributing to a successful program of eradicating sexual harassment is the commitment of the school board president, the board as a whole, individual board members, and the superintendent of schools. "Superintendent Dan Hode gives great support to this policy. He and the board expect all staff and students to be trained in sexual harassment issues. Board members have attended employee sexual harassment training to show their support for the programs."

In order to ensure that all people are aware of the policy, it is posted throughout each school. The posting procedure in each building is left to the discretion of the principal, but typically, the principal provides each teacher with a copy of the posting, and asks that it be posted in each classroom. All support employees are also given copies of the policy.

The district also provides inservice opportunities to employees during the school year. Administrators have been trained by an outside consultant who specializes in sexual harassment issues. Some of the larger buildings and departments have also had outside consultants speak to their staffs. Palin personally trained over six hundred employees in 1993. Each year, every employee is scheduled for some orientation to sexual harassment.

All students are also made aware of the district's policy. Again, the specific procedures and time lines are left to the principal of the individual buildings, but principals are directed to have this policy discussed in all classrooms in age-appropriate ways. Some of the elementary principals personally visit the classrooms to do this. Also, in the upper elementary grades, the students are shown a videotape on the differences between good and bad touching which leads to issues of sexual harassment and encourages students to report concerns they have in this area. The secondary health teachers incorporate sexual harassment awareness in their teaching.

In order to ensure that everyone knows exactly what constitutes sexual harassment, all students and staff members are presented with the following specific examples of sexual harassment at school:

Staff-to-Student Harassment

1. A male teacher placing his arms around middle school girls and rubbing their backs as positive reinforcement for a job well done.

2. A teacher's inquiry into a student's personal, social, and sexual life.

3. Leering or staring at the intimate body parts of a student.

4. A bus driver playing a game with elementary students involving tickling and touching of the students by the bus driver.

5. A teacher showing favoritism towards students who welcome sexually suggestive comments or behavior.

Student-to-Student Harassment

1. Student bra snapping, giving "snuggies" or "pantsing" (pulling down boys' or girls' pants or lifting up girls' skirts).

2. Students "rating" other students.

3. Students displaying or circulating centerfolds or sexually explicit materials.

4. Name calling: "slut," "whore," "fag," "lesbian," "cow," or "dog."

5. Teasing students about their sexual activities or lack of sexual activity.

6. Students wearing sexually offensive t-shirts, hats, or pins.

7. Displays of affection between students (i.e. "making out") in the halls.

8. Suggestive comments about apparel.

Student-to-Staff Harassment

1.   Students making sexually explicit and threatening comments to a staff member.

2.   Students "hiding" sexually explicit materials in a classroom where a teacher will find them.

3.   Students passing around sexually explicit and derogatory illustrations of the principal.

4.   Students making obscene phone calls to a teacher at his or her home.

The South Washington County Schools' policy contains a complaint and investigation procedure. Complaints against students are handled by the building staff. Student discipline may be administered under the student discipline policy. Students have, for example, been removed from school buses for the balance of the school year for sexual harassment incidents on a bus.

Complaints against employees are usually handled by an outside investigator if the complainant is a student, and by the Human Resources Department if the complainant is another employee. Palin's experience is that employees appreciate knowing that they have a way to address these problems, and that their complaints are taken seriously and all parties are treated fairly. This district is confident that sexual harassment has been reduced as a result of a clear policy and fair investigations.

Palin reports that the South Washington County Schools' policy was created to provide a positive working and learning environment, free of sexual harassment. The complaint and investigation procedure provides an opportunity for sexual harassment complaints to be handled quickly, and before they become so serious that they require legal action. Palin is convinced that "the school district and its employees are well treated by this policy, when compared to the costs, delays, notoriety, and stress of going through the courts or other outside agencies."

A Building Level Program to Eradicate Sexual Harassment

Goodrich Middle School in Lincoln, Nebraska, is typical of other schools across the country. The behaviors of its students reflect the values of its community. Several years ago a group of school counselors began to observe some male students violating the physical and psychological safety of female students. These behaviors included comments, gestures, inappropriate public displays of affection, and unwelcome touching. The counselors also noticed that many of the female students did not seem to understand their rights to declare and demand respect for personal boundaries.

The counselors determined that students were receiving mixed signals regarding appropriate and inappropriate behavior. Consequently, a team of guidance counselors developed an age appropriate program that addressed a variety of objectives regarding the issue of sexual harassment.

The program includes a discussion of the definition of sexual harassment. This discussion stresses that sexual harassment is sexual behavior that is, "not welcomed, one-sided, and deals with power." The program also stresses that sexual harassment is a violation of the Lincoln Public School Policy.

The program explains that anyone can be sexually harassed. "This means students, teachers, parents, or others who are part of the school (janitors, bus drivers, office or lunch room staff) may be victims of sexual harassment." Students are reminded that although females are most often the victims, males can also be sexually harassed. The training makes a particular point of reminding the students that victims can be from any ethnic or cultural group. However, the program notes that "people of color experience sexual harassment more often than European Americans."

One of the parts of the program that we particularly like is the section where the students are reminded that people make a choice to harass someone. This emphasizes the student's responsibility for his own behavior and reinforces the fact that students have the power to refrain from harassing. Students are reminded that harassers can be male or female, from any ethnic or cultural group, and may be an adult or another student.

The Goodrich program stresses that sexual harassment is not the victim's fault, is not harmless fun, is not normal sexual attraction, and is not "asked for" by the victim. Students are told that sexual harassment usually does not go away if it is ignored, and it usually gets worse if it's not stopped. The presentation concludes by reaffirming that the Lincoln Public Schools will not tolerate sexual harassment and serious consequences will result if a student is found to have sexually harassed another student. The program includes role playing, and question and answer sessions.

According to counselors Cathy Rauch, Luetta Sandquist, and Ann Stokes, there have been "immediate and long term benefits as a result of this program. Everyone now speaks a 'common language' when discussing the issue of sexual harassment. By talking about the 'unspeakable,' students have been given permission to discuss their concerns and to report incidents of sexual harassment."

Although statistics have not been kept, the counselors and administrators believe that there are significantly fewer instances of inappropriate touching and other forms of sexual harassment as a result of this program. When incidents do occur, the counselors have found it helpful to refer to the classroom presentations when talking to students and parents. Valarie Hubbard-Harris, assistant principal at the school, told us, "It is especially important to have this training with seventh grade students because they are still trying out behaviors in an effort to figure out what is appropriate. These kids really never thought about the topic of sexual harassment. They are still carrying some roughhousing behavior of elementary school as they begin to make the transition to secondary school."

Hubbard-Harris reports that because of this program female students are more willing to come into the office and tell the counselors or principal exactly what happened and what they did about it. "For example, an eighth grade girl came to my office this week and said, 'He grabbed my breast and I told him to take his hands off of me. I came in here to report him.' We are seeing much more assertive behaviors on the part of victims of sexual harassment."

Education Can Make A Difference

We have little or no reason to believe that contentious relations between men and women have any genetic or biological foundation. This rather strongly suggests that conflict is socialized or learned. If this is true, then education can be a powerful catalyst for change. However, a change in culture results from a process in which changes of knowledge and beliefs, changes of values and standards, changes of emotional attachments and needs, and changes in the framework of an individual's total life in the group all take place. In other words, the kind of cultural change required to eradicate sexual harassment in our schools requires not just transference of facts, but significant alteration of the belief system of the culture. In order for programs of sexual harassment eradication to be successful the microcosm of those efforts, group values must be significantly altered. In these cases, the group begins to support different values, making it far easier for each individual to accept these new values. Another pillar of success in these programs is the free expression and open discussion of the problematic attitudes or behavior. In order for change to take place, members of the group must feel free to express openly the very sentiments which we are trying to eradicate.

There is no question that resolving the conflict between boys and girls, men and women will require a large component of reeducation. As we have learned in our review of the above programs, there are numerous and varied ways to achieve this reeducation. The purpose of this chapter has not been to mandate specific solutions but to create an awareness that solutions are possible. We also hope the portrayal of the models included in this discussion will lead to even greater exploration and implementation of innovative ideas and programs.

Value of Training

Training is a big part of most of the programs that are being used to help eradicate sexual harassment from our schools. In 1976 Beauvais conducted a study to evaluate the impact of a training program that was designed to increase students' understanding of what constitutes sexual harassment, to increase participants' sensitivity toward students who were sexually harassed, and to reduce tolerance of all participants for sexually harassing behaviors. In this study male and female college students who were resident hall staff members participated in a two hour training session. During this session the participants looked at a series of six videotapes that illustrated various examples of sexual harassment. The students completed a sexual harassment attitude survey prior to and at the completion of the training session. The participants in this study significantly increased their awareness of sexual harassment issues as a result of the training experience. Interestingly, the women participants did not significantly change their perceptions. However, men dramatically increased their recognition of what behavior constitutes sexual harassment and also increased their sensitivity to students who are harassed.

Although changes in attitudes do not necessarily translate into changes in behaviors, a study conducted by Jones and Jacklin reinforced the belief that training can change students' attitudes about sexual harassment. This study indicated that both male and female college students' sexist attitudes were significantly lowered as the result of an introductory course in gender studies.

From the results of these studies, we conclude that training/education efforts can change attitudes and should be begun early in a child's elementary school education.

Recommendations for Eradicating Sexual Harassment

Now that we have discussed the seriousness of the problem of sexual harassment in our schools, and have shared several examples of how various groups are working to develop stronger self-concepts, reduce gender conflict and eradicate sexual harassment from our schools, we would like to offer several additional recommendations.

Empowerment

One of the most important aspects of sexual harassment prevention is empowerment. Young women must be taught the skills necessary to defend themselves from intimidation and harassment. Schools should empower people to take control of their lives. Programs should strive to build self-esteem and personal skills which allow program students to face problems and interactions in new ways. Boys and girls should learn skills to interact with others in a more productive and appropriate manner. For example, girls who learn assertiveness often use assertive communication skills and develop an attitude of self-respect ("I have the right to be treated with respect and dignity.") which leads them to stop sexual harassment they encounter, or at least to realize that such behavior is not acceptable. Programs which help men learn to treat others with respect and dignity include communication skills and positive interaction skills. Thus, they learn productive, appropriate, and legal methods of interacting with females. Such programs hold promise for preventing and stopping individual sexual harassment.

Some of the following recommendations are adapted from a follow-up study on sexual harassment that was conducted by Merit System Protection Board. Others are adapted from suggestions offered by Claire Walsh.

Recommendation #1
Examine The School Environment

A.   Examine your school's educational climate with an eye to identifying its hostility to females. Before you begin making policies and rules and regulations you must find out what is going on in your school or school district. Your policy should be responsive to the unique nature of your community, while at the same time ensuring that all students are protected from sexual harassment. Although we have provided several sample policies, we do not recommend that you adopt these or others without carefully examining them.

B.   When you are looking at your educational environment, be sure you look at the behavior of teachers, administrators, classified staff, and school board members. As official representatives of the school district, behavior in the teacher's lounge, the golf course, or while attending educational conferences reflects the image and climate of the school district. Professional educators must model non-sexist behavior and eradicate sexual harassment from their own lives.

Recommendation #2
Initiate a Task Force On Sexual Harassment

A.   The issue of sexual harassment should not be addressed in a vacuum. Although we can understand why some school administrators are reluctant to discuss this issue with the public, this fear is not well-founded. Sexual harassment is not a school problem. It is a community problem. Each community has a wealth of often untapped resources that can help the school develop appropriate, accurate and effective programs to eradicate sexual harassment. The task force should include representatives from community groups, law enforcement agencies, rape crisis advocates, children's service agencies, and other community organizations, as well as parents, teachers, administrators, and students.

Recommendation #3
Policy Statements

A.   Every school district should have a specific policy statement that prohibits all forms of sexual harassment. In order to be effective, this policy must be widely publicized and detail the specific actions that constitute sexual harassment and define the penalties for each of the actions.

B.   The sexual harassment policy should be annually evaluated, modified if necessary, and reissued. A policy imbedded in a policy manual does little to eradicate harassment or to assist in a defense to charges of sexual harassment.

C.   The policy must make it clear that sexual harassment is against the law and that the school district will not tolerate it.

D.   The policy should be adopted by the board of education and signed by the board president and by the superintendent of schools.

E.   The policy should define the various behaviors that may constitute sexual harassment including a description of activities that may create a hostile environment.

F.   The policy should include the range of penalties the school district can levy against the harasser, from warning to dismissal or expulsion. It should also discuss the possibility of personal liability for unlawful acts of harassment.

**Recommendation #4
Training**

A.   Each school district should tailor their training/education programs to the individual needs of each segment of the school community. For training efforts to succeed, school districts must provide all administrators, teachers, classified staff, students, and parents with more than generic warnings that sexual harassment is improper. All members of the school community must be taught exactly what constitutes sexual harassment and they must be sensitized to understand and recognize what they can do to eradicate sexual harassment.

B.   Training sessions should be developed and presented for parents and other community members.

C.   All employees, students, and parents must be convinced that sexual harassment can be deemed illegal and that strong sanctions can, and will, be applied to any member of the school community who is responsible for such behavior.

D.   All members of the administration, teaching, and support staff should be required to take sexual harassment training.   All students should have at least one session in which sexual harassment is defined and the consequences for the harasser and the victim are clearly explained.

E.   The training should thoroughly cover the range of possible behaviors and the circumstances under which those behaviors may be considered sexual harassment, the formal and informal actions for seeking relief, the right to confidentiality under certain circumstances for those alleging harassment, the prohibition of reprisals, and current case law relevant to sexual harassment.

F.   All new employees should receive training early in their employment. All students should receive training early in the school year.

G.   The training program should be periodically evaluated for effectiveness.

H.   Don't separate males from females during training sessions. All employees and all students must receive the same information about this topic. Both males and females have the same rights and responsibilities. By separating them you perpetuate the misconception that most men are guilty of harassment, that only women are victims, and that this is a divisive issue, a battle of the sexes.

Recommendation #5
Complaint and Investigation Procedures

A.   Simply having a sexual harassment policy and training program does not necessarily insulate a school district from liability. In order to be effective, the policy must include a grievance procedure that encourages victims of harassment to come forward.

B.   There should be both a formal and informal avenue of redress available to employees who believe they are victims of sexual harassment. The school district must have a mechanism in place that allows it to quickly institute any needed reforms.

C.   The process should be timely, ensure reasonable confidentiality, and protect the victim from any reprisals. A goal of 120 days to resolve any complaint is reasonable.

Recommendation #6
Enforcement Action

A.   All faculty, staff, and students must clearly understand that the school district has a strong and effective system of sanctions against sexual harassment. They must know that   all accusations of sexual harassment will be investigated and if a person is found to be guilty of sexual harassment there will be strong and appropriate penalties.

B.   The school district should publicize the specific information about the penalties harassers face.

Recommendation #7
Additional Prevention Efforts

A.   The school district should conduct periodic, random, anonymous surveys to determine whether sexual harassment is a problem in a given department, building, or classroom.

B.   An evaluation/prevention effort should include conducting periodic follow-up interviews with all personnel involved in the settlement of both informal and formal complaints.

C.   Administrators should assess the current school environment of the employees involved in harassment complaints to ensure that problems relating to that sexual harassment incident no longer exist.

School districts that begin to face and solve the problems of sexual harassment need to be supported by their communities. This process is often painful and may sometimes be embarrassing. New attitudes and behaviors must be developed. Parents must be willing to help their local educators as they create and enforce new policies. It has been our experience that as students and teachers come to understand sexual harassment and trust the school systems' willingness and ability to respond to complaints, there may be an increase in reports of sexual harassment. This is an indication that students trust the school enough to openly address sexual harassment.

Education does not create more harassment. It puts a name on the inappropriate behavior that may already exist. Education does not create more problems for educators. It allows existing problems to be identified and solved at the local level. It is our hope that by joining in partnership with the schools, parents can help the schools eradicate sexual harassment without having to resort to the legal system.

Chapter Seven

Anatomy of a Sexual Harassment Hearing

Each incident of sexual harassment will, of course, be different, and all investigations must be conducted in a manner that is consistent with your school's policy and procedures. We recommend that all of the material in this book serve as a framework upon which your school district, in consultation with your school attorney, may construct a policy that will meet the needs of your community.

We offer the following material in the hope that it will help you think through the process of conducting an investigation. All of the facts in the following example are taken from actual events. The material has been modified to protect the anonymity of the individuals and the school districts involved.

Suggestions for Conducting a Due Process Hearing on a Sexual Harassment Charge

A Sample Agenda for a Due Process Hearing

1. Introduction:

   Introduce members of the committee

   Identify the parties

2. Advise the parties as to the purpose of the hearing.

Example:

The committee on deportment will consider the proposal of (name of principal), the Principal of Sunflower Middle School requesting the expulsion of (name of student) as a student at Sunflower Middle School for the remainder of the 1993-1994 school year for an alleged violation of the Sexual Harassment Policy of Sunflower School District. The proposal alleges that on or about (date incident happened) (name of students) (name specifically what the student allegedly did).

3.   Explain procedure:
   A.   The principal or designated representative will present evidence in support of the proposal.
   B.   The alleged harasser or designated representative will be allowed to question witness testifying in support of the principal's proposal.
   C.   The alleged harasser or designated representative will be allowed to present witnesses on his/her behalf and may also testify.
   D.   The principal or designated representative will be allowed to question witnesses testifying on his/her behalf.
   E.   Committee members will be allowed to question any witness called upon the completion of the testimony of the principal and the alleged harasser called after their testimony and the student and principal's examination is concluded.
   F.   The principal and alleged harasser, or their representatives will be allowed to make a closing statement to the committee.

G.   The committee will then make a decision.

4.   Inform the parties that the chair will decide any issues of procedure, not lawyers. All will have chance to tell their stories.

5.   Swear in all people that will be testifying. **Oath**--Do you solemnly swear (or affirm) that the testimony you will give before the Committee on Deportment in this matter will be the truth, the whole truth, and nothing but the truth.

6.   Ask the principal and alleged harasser, or their representatives, if they have any opening remarks.

7.   Ask the principal or designated representative to present witnesses and evidence in support of the proposal. (After witness is examined by the principal or designated representative allow the alleged harasser or representative the right to question. Thereafter let principal's representative question if he/she desires and student's representative to do likewise. Then allow committee members to question).

8.   After principal's witnesses have testified, allow alleged harasser or representative to call designated witnesses and present evidence. Follow the same process as when principal's witnesses testify.

9.   After witnesses on both sides have presented their testimonies, take closing remarks from principal's

representative and alleged harasser's representative. (The chair has the right to set a time limit for closing remarks.)

10.　　After closing remarks have been made the Chair announces that the committee will deliberate and reach a decision. Ask parties and witnesses to leave the room until this is done. However, they should stay available. The committee deliberates and determines whether :

A.　　The evidence supports the principal's proposal and (name of student) is expelled as a student at Sunflower for the remainder of the 1993-1994 school year;

B.　　The evidence does not support the principal's proposal that (name of student) should be expelled as a student at Sunflower School for the remainder of the 1993-1994 school year.

During deliberation the committee must pay close attention to the school district's policy. The issue is whether, based on the evidence presented, the principal's proposal is reasonable and justified. When the committee has made a determination, the chair is responsible for sending a letter to the superintendent and the student stating the decision. The following is a sample of such a letter:

Letter Reporting The Findings Of The Committee on Deportment

You are advised that the Committee on Deportment appointed by Superintendent Good to consider the proposal of Principal Wright of Sunflower Middle School an attendance center in such district, for expulsion of (name of student) therein met on the (date of hearing) commencing at (time, date and location).

The members of the Committee on Deportment were the following certified employees of the district:

(Name the persons, the positions and the schools they serve) All members of the committee were present.

The parties appearing were: (Name of all parties and position)

The committee reviewed the file in this matter and found that notice of the hearing was given to (name of student) as required by law and the policies of the district.

Evidence was presented on behalf of the principal's proposal, the alleged harasser's witnesses, and closing statements made. Based on the evidence presented at the hearing the committee determined that:

A. The incident occurred on (date).

B. The facts were stated

C. By engaging in the aforesaid conduct (name of student) violated (sections of the BOE policy)

D. There is substantial evidence to support the principal's recommendation that (name of student) be expelled as a student from (name of school) an attendance center within the district for the remainder of the (dates) school year and that such expulsion is reasonable and justified.

E. The expulsion of (name of student) as a student of Sunflower Middle School shall continue until any appeal from this committee's decision is determined or until the period of expulsion has expired, whichever is sooner.

The decision of the committee as set out above is adopted by a vote of _____ for and ____ against.

Dated this _____ at _____ o'clock.

_____

Signatures of all committee members

Sample Report of A Sexual Harassment Hearing

Brandon is an eighth-grade student at Sunflower Middle School. As a result of various, ongoing incidents involving inappropriate behavior and language throughout the 1993-94 school year, Brandon was suspended from school for a period of five days and a due process hearing was held pursuant to the school district policy. Brandon and his parents were given written notice of the time and place of the hearing and of the charge against him. He was charged with violation of the Student Conduct Policy Prohibiting Sexual Harassment.

The hearing was held on Tuesday, April 20, 1994, at 8:05 p.m., in the Board of Education meeting room, of the school district administration building. Brandon appeared with his parents, Mr. and Mrs. Ralph Williams. He was not represented by counsel. Brandon was advised of his right to counsel and waived same. Brandon was informed that he had the right to testify or not to testify, to cross-examine witnesses against him and to present his own witnesses.

Ms. Jackie Easterlake, Esquire, represented the school board. Mr. Steve Starkley, middle school principal, attended the hearing on behalf of the administration. The entire school board has familiarized itself with the record and conducted the hearing.

Finding of Fact

1.   Student Brandon Williams committed various acts of sexual harassment by words and actions during the current school year and in the presence of students and teachers.

2.   Student Brandon Williams' words constituting sexual harassment took the following forms:

   a.   Asked a man jogging on the school track, "Why is your anus called Uranus?"

   b.   Said to a teacher, "It smells like old pussy in here."

   c.   Repeatedly said during homeroom, "Blow job."

   d.   Said to a female student, "Close your legs so I don't have to look at you."

   e.   Suggested to a female student that she would enjoy sitting on an aquarium pump because of the vibrating motion when it was in use.

   f.   Said in the presence of a teacher that he had anal intercourse with his girlfriend.

   g.   Asked female students to spread their legs so that he could have a better look.

   h.   Remarked in science class, when the teacher drew a mushroom on the board, that it looked like an erection.

   i.   Shouted across the room, to ask a male student whether he had a particular brand of condoms.

   k.   Referred to parts of female students' anatomies in sexual terms.

   l.   Took innocent comments made by others and turn them into sexual innuendos or made sexually suggestive comments using the words.

3.   Student Brandon Williams committed the following acts which are forms of sexual harassment:

   a.   Lay on the floor and moved his hips in a sexual gesture.

   b.   When working with meter sticks, placed the stick between his legs like a penis and exhibited this to other students.

   c.   Placed rulers between his legs indicating that they were his penis and made a masturbating motion with his hand.

4.   Student Brandon Williams' above words and actions were directed at specific individuals, both students and faculty, or to no one in particular.

5.   Student Brandon Williams' activities were often done blatantly enough that all in the classroom could hear or see.

6.   Brandon Williams' actions tended to inhibit, intimidate, and harass students and faculty in the following ways:

   a.   When Brandon would take the innocent comments of others and turn them into sexual innuendos, teachers became fearful of using any word that could be misconstrued, and female students tended to retreat from classroom participation.

   b.   When the Brandon was in a class, students and the teacher sensed an underlying tension because Brandon was frequently combative toward others.

7.   At the hearing, Brandon totally denied all of the allegations against him.

8.   The student's attendance record is good.

9.   The student's academic record is very poor.

10.   The student's disciplinary record this year is poor. The
       record indicates that he has been disciplined five different
       times for various offenses including class disruption,
       incidents on the bus, and acts of sexual harassment.

Conclusion

1.   The charge against the student is sustained and supported by
      sufficient evidence of record.
2.   Brandon Williams engaged in acts which constitute
      misconduct within the meaning of the Student Conduct
      Policy Prohibiting Sexual Harassment.
3.   The conduct of the student did cause and warrants a
      conclusion that his continued presence in school would cause
      a serious threat to the health, safety and welfare of the
      students and employees of the Sunflower School District.
4.   Now therefore, this day, 1994, the Board of Education of
      Sunflower School District hereby determines that Brandon
      Williams, Student Number 000-00-0000:
      1.   Is hereby expelled from the Sunflower Schools
      2.   May be readmitted to the Sunflower Schools upon
            a.   receipt of evidence satisfactory to the
                  Administration that the behavior described
                  above has been corrected and
            b.   receipt of a petition for reinstatement
                  submitted by his parents.

Board of Education of the Sunflower School District
By: _____   Attest:_____
President   Secretary

Sample Letter To School Superintendent

Date

Dr. Joe Smith
Superintendent of Schools
Sunflower School District
Sunflower, USA

Dear Dr. Smith:

Enclosed please find the report of the Committee on Deportment concerning the hearing involving the proposal of Principal X for the expulsion of Brandon Williams as a student at such attendance center.

Sincerely,

Name of chairperson
Committee on Deportment

Discipline

Finally, any investigation must be followed by significant action to prevent future harassment. In addition, appropriate disciplinary and punitive sanctions must be levied against the harasser. Without strong sanctions against the harasser, students and staff, will consider the policy prohibiting sexual harassment to be a hoax. The severity of such sanctions should be proportional to the severity of the offense.

Part Two
Curriculum Guides

Introduction

Goals of The Curriculum

It is essential all teachers and students understand that sexual harassment harms people and will not be tolerated. They should understand that sexual harassment is illegal. They should understand that sexual harassment is wrong in spite of innocent intent.

The U. S. Supreme Court has made it clear that educators are responsible for ensuring that sexual harassment and other forms of discrimination are eradicated from our schools.

The goals of the curriculum are to:

1. Development of self-esteem and the self-esteem of others.

2. Help young students develop an awareness of the consequences of inappropriate behavior

3. Help students to recognize sexual harassment and articulate the differences between a compliment, flirtation and sexual harassment.

4.   Inform students of their legal rights and responsibilities regarding sexual harassment.

5.   Inform students of appropriate ways to respond to incidents of sexual harassment.

6.   Promote an understanding of the dynamics of sexual harassment as a social problem.

The activities have been prepared for grades K-12 and focus on sexual harassment rather than sexual discrimination or sexism in general. At the secondary level, these activities are designed to be included with course work in related areas such as social studies, sociology, women's studies, career education, health courses, vocational education courses and family studies.

We call to your attention two other curriculum guides: *Sexual Harassment To Teenagers* published by the Minnesota Department of Education and *Who's Hurt and Whose Liable?: Sexual Harassment in Massachusetts Schools* published by the Massachusetts Department of Education.

How to use this curriculum guide.

Why use a curriculum guide? A school district should have a curriculum guide and/or training to support their policies. School districts have, for example, general policies for writing curriculum, textbook adoption, and hiring of personnel. A school district that adopts a sexual harassment policy, must ensure that students and staff have the information necessary understand the causes, consequences and strategies for prevention of sexual harassment.

The K-3 curriculum guide deals with recognizing and appreciating individual differences, accepting responsibility for behavior, and identifying of good and bad touches. In the 4-6 curriculum guide, the same concepts are presented with the addition of defining and understanding sexual harassment. The curriculum guide for Grades 7-12 deals exclusively with the concept of sexual harassment.

The curriculum guide identifies teaching material, time allotment, suggested grade level and learning activities. The materials in the curriculum guides are presented in three sections: Grades K-3, Grades 4-6 and Grades 7-12. Each curriculum guide provides a sequence of activities using specific goals and objectives. Teachers may use the material as a unit or use it at various times during the course of the school year. Teachers may use it as a guide to complement any existing programs or materials. In order to be able to appropriately use this curriculum guide it is necessary to first become familiar with the background material presented in the previous chapters of this book.

Chapter Eight

Curriculum Guide For Grades K-3

Goal:

    1.   To improve students' ability to make responsible decisions.

Objectives:

    1.   To understand and appreciate one's own uniqueness and accept differences in others.

    2.   To understand and accept responsibility for one's own behavior.

    3.   To understand "good touch/bad touch" and identify appropriate times to say "no."

Activity # 1

Goal:	To improve students' ability to make responsible decisions.
Objective:	To understand and appreciate your own individual uniqueness and accepting differences in others.
Group:	Grades K-3
Time:	30-45 minutes
Materials:	Butcher paper, crayons, scissors

This is an activity that will take several days to complete. Discussion time will take between 30 and 45 minutes depending on the size of your class.

Directions: Trace around the body of each child on butcher paper. The teacher may have to do this for each child or put the children in pairs and they can take turns tracing their bodies. Each child can cut around the tracing or leave it as is. Instruct each child to draw in their features (i.e. brown hair, glasses, blue eyes, dark skin, shirt, jeans, etc.) It might take students as long as a week to complete, but they can work on their pictures when they have free time. At the end of the week when the pictures are completed, discuss the differences between the students.

Ask the following questions: How are the pictures alike? How are they different? How many students have blonde hair, brown hair, red hair? How many different colors of eyes do we have in our room? Does anybody in this room have a characteristic (something that is different from anybody else) that makes them better than another person--why or why not?

Activity # 2

Goal:	To improve students' ability to make responsible decisions.
Objective:	To understand and appreciate one's own individual uniqueness and accept differences in others.
Group:	Grades K-3
Time:	30 minutes
Materials:	*Gertrude McFuzz* by Dr. Seuss

Synopsis--*Gertrude McFuzz* is approximately third and fourth grade reading level with 15 pages. This is a story about a bird named Gertrude McFuzz. She was not pleased with her tail because it was very small and plain. Gertrude liked the tail that Lolla-Lee-Lou (another bird) had and would do anything to get one.

Read the story *Gertrude McFuzz* to the class and use the following questions for discussion.

Stop after Gertrude eats two berries and ask: After Gertrude takes the berry to grow her tail, she decides that two berries would work better. What do you think will happen to Gertrude? Why do you think that Gertrude was so concerned about her tail? Do you think that Gertrude will be satisfied with three tails?

Stop after Gertrude eats three dozen berries and ask: What do you think will happen to Gertrude when she eats all of the berries? If she grows many tails, do you think it will cause her any problems?

At the end of the story ask these questions. Why couldn't Gertrude fly? Why was Gertrude so concerned about looking like Lolla-Lee-Lou? Do you think other birds made fun the way she looked? How does it make you feel when somebody makes fun of you or calls you names? What should you do when that happens? When Gertrude grew a tail and she looked like Lolla-Lee-Lou, why wasn't she satisfied with the way she looked? How are we different or alike (i.e. hair, eyes, do you wear glasses, girls or boys)?

Activity # 3

Goal: To improve students' ability to make responsible decisions.

Objective: To understand and appreciate one's own individual uniqueness and accept differences in others.

Group: Grades K-3

Time: 30 minutes

Materials: *Blueberries For Sal* by Robert McCloskey

Synopsis--*Blueberries for Sal* is approximately upper second grade to third grade reading level with 28 pages of actual text. Every page has illustrations which will keep a child's interest. The longest text on any one page consists of 10 lines. *Blueberries for Sal* is a Caldecott Honor Book. The book is about a little girl who helps her mother pick blueberries for canning. During the outing with her mother, Sal gets lost and ends up with a bear.

Before reading the story *Blueberries For Sal*, show the students the pictures of Sal and ask the following questions:

What is Sal wearing? Do you think Sal is a girl or a boy? Why do you think Sal is a girl? Why do you think Sal is a boy? (Various comments may influence what the students think--i.e. haircut, overalls, name, helping mother, etc.) Could a girl wear overalls, help mother, have a short haircut? Could a boy?

Discover that Sal is a girl as you read the story. Point out at the end of the story that Sal could just as easily been a boy.

Additional activities--Discussion of non-traditional jobs for men and women could be discussed. If some students think that certain jobs are exclusively male or female, ask in a person who works in that job to speak to your class or take the class to the job site and show them men and women working together.

Activity # 4

Goal: To improve students' ability to make responsible decisions.

Objective: To understand and appreciate one's own individual uniqueness and accept differences in others.

Group: Grades K-3

Time: 20-30 minutes

Materials: *William's Doll* by Charlotte Zolotow

Synopsis--*William's Doll* is approximately upper second grade to third grade reading level with 32 pages. The book is colorfully illustrated, but the pictures are small and it would be difficult to show a large classroom of children. William is a little boy that would like to have a doll, but his father and brother don't like the idea.

Read the story *William's Doll* to the class and use the following questions for discussion.

Ask the following questions after you read the story. What did William's brother and the boy next door say to William when he said he wanted a doll? When William's father found out that he wanted a doll, what did he do? Did William like the new basketball that his father bought for him? Did William like the electric train his father bought for him? When William told his grandmother that he wanted a doll, what was her reaction? Is it important to be a good father? How does your father help take care of you?

Activity # 5

Goal: To improve students' ability to make responsible decisions.

Objective: To understand and appreciate one's own individual uniqueness and accept differences in others.

Group: Grades K-3

Time: 15-20 minutes

Materials: *Leo The Late Bloomer* by Robert Kraus

Synopsis--*Leo The Late Bloomer* is approximately upper first grade to second grade reading level with 28 pages. The book is colorfully illustrated with large pictures adequate to show a large class. Leo is tiger that can't do anything right. His mother isn't worried because she knows that Leo is just a "late bloomer".

Read the book *Leo The Late Bloomer* by Robert Kraus. Ask the following questions after the book is read.

Ask the following questions after you read the story. Could Leo do anything right? What were some of the things that Leo couldn't do? His father was very concerned, but what did Leo's mother say? What does "late-bloomer" mean? Can all of the students in our room do the same thing? Why or why not? Can you name something that another classmate can do very well? Would you make fun of somebody if they couldn't do everything well? How would you help them? Would you say something if another classmate was being teased? What would you do?

Activity # 6

Goal:	To improve students' ability to make responsible decisions.
Objective:	To understand and appreciate one's own uniqueness and accept differences in others.
Group:	Grades K-3
Time:	15-45 minutes
Materials:	*A Country Far Away* by Nigel Gray

Synopsis--*A Country Far Away* is approximately upper first grade to second grade reading level with 26 pages. Every page is colorfully illustrated with no more than one line of text per page. The side-by-side illustrations show similarities between two boys, one in a western country and the other in a rural African village.

Read *A Country Far Away* and have the students compare the two different cultures. The teacher should guide the students through the activity by asking the students to discuss the differences in the illustrations. Ask how are these families different from your family?

Students can illustrate their own books by using the same text from *A Country Far Away* showing what their families are like. This can be done in one class period or the story may be read one day and the illustrations on another day. Have each student tell the class about their book and identify and discuss the differences between the students in the classroom?

Activity # 7

Goal:	To improve students' ability to make responsible decisions.
Objective:	To understand and appreciate one's own uniqueness and accept differences in others.
Group:	Grades K-3
Time:	15-20 minutes
Materials:	*Goggles!* by Ezra Jack Keats

Synopsis--*Goggles!* is approximately second grade reading level with 30 pages. The book, illustrated by the author, depicts city streets and city children. Peter has discovered a pair of motorcycle goggles. As Archie and Peter go off to play with their new treasure, they run into trouble with some older boys.

Ask the following questions after you read the story. Archie and Willie were able to fool the big boys. What could have happened if Willie and Archie had not been able to escape? If you are ever in a situation where you might get hurt, what would you do? What are some other options?

Activity # 8

Goal:	To improve students' ability to make responsible decisions.
Objective:	To understand and accept responsibility for one's behavior.
Group:	Grades K-3
Time:	15-20 minutes
Materials:	*Butterfingers* by Dennis Reader

Synopsis--*Butterfingers* by Dennis Reader is approximately upper second grade to third grade reading level with 24 pages. Every page has colored illustrations with no more than 4 lines of reading on each page. *Butterfingers* is about a little boy named Benjamin who can't do anything right until he gets a very special gift. The teacher needs to allow time for the students to look at the pictures to discover what happens to Benjamin.

Ask the following questions as the story is being read. What happens when Benjamin gathers the eggs for Grandad Butters? What happens when Benjamin slops the hog and milks the cow? Do you think Benjamin will drop his baby sister on the floor when he holds her? Why didn't Benjamin drop his baby sister? Do you think Benjamin's uncles, aunts and grandparents were nervous when Benjamin wanted to hold his baby sister? Why? How do you think it made Benjamin feel when he held his sister? Do you have any brothers or sisters? Do you treat them nicely? Do they treat you nicely? Name some things that you do with your brothers and sisters. Name some things that you do as a family.

Activity # 9

Goal:	To improve students' ability to make responsible decisions.
Objective:	To understand and accept responsibility for your own behavior.
Group:	Grades K-3
Time:	30-45 minutes
Materials:	*Nobody Looks Like Eugene* by Florence Kramon

Synopsis--*Nobody Looks Like Eugene* is approximately upper second grade to third grade reading level with 31 pages. Children will enjoy reading and listening to the book because it rhymes. The book is colorfully illustrated showing all of Eugene's antics. Each person has qualities that are uniquely their own. Eugene G. is a little boy who explores doing things in a new way. The adults in his life handle the new behavior in an unusual way.

Read the story and ask questions after reading each of the following pages:

p. 7	When Eugene G. stood on his head to eat breakfast, how did his parents react?
p. 9	How did Eugene G.'s father act when he washed his face, ears and neck with toothpaste?
p. 11	Did Eugene G.'s grandmother get mad at him when he wore mittens on his feet? What did she say?
p. 13	Did Officer B. laugh at Eugene G. when he stuck the pencils in his ears?
p. 15	Eugene G.'s teacher didn't get mad when he wore his glasses on his ear. What would your teacher say if you did the same thing?
p. 17	When Eugene G. sat on the table to eat dinner how did his parents react?

p. 19 How did they react when he slept under the bed?

p. 20 List all of the things Eugene G. did that day on the board. What would your parents, grandparents, police officer, and teacher say if you acted like Eugene G.?

Finish the story and discuss why Eugene G. acted the way he did. Do you think his friends noticed how silly he acted in class? What would you do if somebody in your classroom was acting that way? Name some better ways to get attention from your parents, teacher or friends.

Activity # 10

Goal:	To improve responsible decision making skills of all students.
Objective:	To understand and accept responsibility for your own behavior.
Group:	Grades K-3
Time:	15-20 minutes
Materials:	*The Zax* by Dr. Seuss

Synopsis--*The Zax* is approximately third or fourth grade reading level with 8 pages. Children of all ages love to read and listen to the silly names and rhymes of Dr. Seuss. It is a great story about two people who are not willing to compromise. Review directions of north and south. Children will have to have some knowledge of directions to understand the meaning or the story.

Read *The Zax* and use the following questions for discussion.

Stop reading after the North-Going Zax declares that he isn't going to move for 59 days and ask the following questions. Why do you think the North-Going Zax is being so stubborn? What do you think the South-Going Zax will say when the North-Going Zax won't move for 59 days?

Stop reading after the South-Going Zax says that he won't budge and the whole world can stand still. Will the whole world stand still just because they won't compromise? What would have been a better way to solve the problem? Do you think the Zaxs missed out on a lot by just standing face to face and not solving their problems? Why? When you have a problem with a friend or classmate, how do you solve it? When you get angry with an adult (your teacher, principal, parents or grandparents) what do you do?

Activity # 11

Goal:	To improve responsible decision making skills of all students.
Objective:	To understand and appreciate the difference between good touch/bad touch and appropriate times to say "no".
Group:	Grades K-3
Time:	30 minutes
Materials:	None

Open the discussion with what is a good touch and what is a bad touch or uncomfortable feeling. What kind of touch makes you feel happy? (i.e. when your parents hug you, when your teacher pats you on the back and says good job, when you're sitting on your parents lap and they read you a story).

Make a list of the suggestions on the board .

Is there any time when a person that you don't know well can touch you and it's all right? (i.e. the school nurse takes your temperature, when the dentist checks your teeth, when the doctor is giving you a check up, in emergency situations where people may be helping you--firefighter, police officer or paramedics)

Make a list of the suggestions on the board.

When is it not okay for somebody to touch you? Listen to your feelings and if it makes you feel uncomfortable, tell a responsible adult (i.e. when a relative wants you to keep a secret and it confuses you, when a stranger or somebody you know touches you in a place that makes you feel uncomfortable.)

Make a list of the suggestions on the board.

Introduce children to the adults in the school building that they can go and talk to if they have a problem and make sure they know where their offices are located. (i.e. School nurse, principal, counselor, social worker)

Bibliography for K-3 Curriculum

A Country Far Away, (1988), by Nigel Gray, Orchard Books.

Blueberries For Sal, (1987), by Robert McCloskey, (Caldecott Honor Book), Penguin Books Ltd.

Butterfingers, (1991), by Dennis Reader, Houghton Mifflin Company.

Gertrude McFuzz by Dr. Seuss, in a collection of stories **Six by Seuss,** (1991), Random House

Goggles!, (1969),by Ezra Jack Keats, (Runner-up for the Caldecott Medal), Macmillan Company.

Leo The Late Bloomer, (1971), by Robert Kraus, Windmill Books.

Nobody Looks Like Eugene, (1967), by Florence Kramon, Follett Publishing Company.

The Zax, by Dr. Seuss, in a collection of stories **The Sneetches and Other Stories**, (1961), Random House

William's Doll, (1972), by Charlotte Zolotow, Harper and Row.

Chapter Nine

Curriculum Guide For Grades 4-6

Goals:

1. To improve responsible decision making skills of all students.

2. To increase awareness of sexual harassment.

Objectives:

1. To understand and appreciate one's own individual uniqueness and accept differences in others.

2. To understand and accept responsibility for your own behavior.

3. To understand "good touch/bad touch" and identify appropriate times to say "no".

4. Define and understand sexual harassment.

Activity # 1

Goal: To improve students' ability to make responsible decisions.

Objective: To understand and appreciate one's own uniqueness and accept differences in others.

Group: Grades 4-6

Time: 15-20 minutes

Materials: Bulletin board space and table

Feature one student a week throughout the school year and let them bring things from home that tell or show something about them and their family (i.e. pictures, hobbies, a essay on their life, time line of their life). They can put the display on the bulletin board or display things on the table that tell the class about themselves. The teacher should allow at least 15 minutes for the student to explain the display. Each student should be allowed to keep their display in the room for the whole week.

Every month take time to discuss the four students that had displays. What were some of the differences between the students? Tell something good about each student. Is there something that each student has worked on to improve? Each student can list some personal goals for improvement. Have any of the students had some problems that the entire class can solve? What are the suggestions?

Activity # 2

Goal: To improve students' ability to make responsible decisions.

Objective: To understand and accept responsibility for one's own behavior.

Group: Grades 4-6

Time: 30-45 minutes

Materials: *My Way Sally* by Mindy Bingham and Penelope Colville Paine
Activity Sheet, pencil.

Synopsis--rt*My Way Sally* is approximately fourth grade reading level. It is a beautifully illustrated big book which depicts the English countryside. The story is about a foxhound named Sally. She forms a friendship with a fox which leads her to doubt whether she wants to be leader of the fox hunt someday. As she explores her options, she trains herself to lead the fox hunt in a new way.

Before reading the story ask the students to write down one or two thoughts for questions 4,5, and 6 on the activity sheet.

Read the story *My Way Sally* to the class and use the remaining questions on the activity sheet to stimulate discussion.

Divide the class into groups of 3-6. Ask the groups to go over each student's statements on questions 4, 5, and 6. Ask the groups to go over each student's statement on questions 4,5 and 6 and form some consensus.

Activity Sheet
My Way Sally

1. When Sally went out with the older dogs on the fox hunt and caught the scent of the fox, why did she run back to the manor house?

2. What options did Sally have if she didn't chase the fox?

3. Sally turned out to be a leader in a different way. How did she prepare for her work and what was the end result?

4. If you saw somebody doing something wrong or something you didn't agree with, what would you do? Would you go along with the crowd or would you do something different?

5. Write an example of something that has happened at school or home that you didn't think was right. How did you handle the situation? How did the adults respond to the situation?

6. If you were a world leader, how would you solve this problem? (Teacher selected current issue.)

Activity # 3

Goal:	To improve students' ability to make responsible decisions.
Objective:	To understand and accept responsibility for one's own behavior.
Group:	Grades 4-6
Time:	30 minutes
Materials:	*The Big Brag* by Dr. Seuss

Synopsis--*The Big Brag* is approximately third or fourth grade reading level with 30 pages. It is a story about a bear and a rabbit who each thought they had qualities that made them in the world making them superior to everybody else.

Read *The Big Brag* and answer the use the following questions for discussion.

Stop reading after the rabbit declares that his ears are the best and ask: Why do you think the rabbit wants to be the best? What do you think the bear will say?

Stop reading after the bear says his "smeller's so keen that it just can't be beat" and ask: Which one is better--the bear or the rabbit? Why? Since both have qualities of equal value, how are they going to solve their problems?

At the end of the story ask: Who won? Who was the wisest character in the story? Do you think some of the characters in the story exaggerated their qualities? It's all right to feel good about yourself and to be able to do things better than anybody else, but should you brag? How will this make your friends or classmates feel toward you?

Activity # 4

Goal:	To improve students' ability to make responsible decisions.
Objective:	To understand and accept responsibility for one's own behavior.
Group:	Grades 4-6
Time:	30 minutes
Materials:	*The Sneetches* by Dr. Seuss

Synopsis--The Sneetches is approximately a third grade reading level with 25 pages. There are Star-Belly Sneetches and Plain-Belly Sneetches. The star is the only identifying mark that makes them different. The Star-Belly Sneetches won't have anything to do with the Plain-Belly Sneetches and that is where all of the trouble begins.

Read the *Sneetches* and use the following questions for discussion.

Stop after the statement "And that's how they treated them year after year." Ask these questions: Why did the Star-Belly Sneetches treat the Plain-Belly Sneetches the way they did? How does it make you feel when somebody won't let you participate in a game? What do you think can be done to make the Sneetches get along together?

At the end of the story ask these questions: What was Sylvester McMonkey McBean's role in the story? Did he help the Sneetches solve their problems?--why not? How did the Sneetches finally solve their problem? If somebody is treating you in a way that makes you feel badly, how do you handle it? How would you treat somebody that has a different skin color or believes in a different religion? What are the consequences of discrimination? People that have great courage will say something when they see something wrong. Will you have the courage to say something or will you just follow the crowd?

Activity # 5

Goal:	To improve students' ability to make responsible decisions.
Objective:	To understand and accept responsibility for one's own behavior.
Group:	Grades 4-6
Time:	30-45 minutes
Materials:	*Molly's Pilgrim* by Barbara Cohen

Synopsis--*Molly's Pilgrim* is approximately a fourth grade reading level. It is illustrated in black and white with 28 pages. Molly wants to go back to Russia because the children in school tease her about being Jewish, her imperfect English and her old-country clothes. Molly's mother reminds her why they immigrated from Russia and Molly learns what a modern Pilgrim is.

Ask the following questions after you read the story. Why didn't Molly's classmates like her? What had she done to her classmates? Do you ever tease a classmate? Why? Do you help another student when they are being teased by another classmate? Why or why not? How would you help? How did Molly's mother react when Molly was being teased? Why didn't Molly want her mother to go to school and talk to her teacher? How did Molly's teacher respond to the students when they teased Molly? How does your teacher respond when you are being teased? Most of the teasing happened on the playground and on Molly's way home from school. Who could help Molly the most with this problem?

When Molly's mother made the Pilgrim, what did Molly think? Was Molly's Pilgrim like one that you have seen? Why was Molly reluctant to take the Pilgrim to school? How did Molly's teacher respond to the Pilgrim?

Additional activities--Have the students find out their family backgrounds and see what countries their ancestors came from. Can the students find out why their ancestors came to America? Students might want to develop a list of questions to use in interviewing relatives, or find old pictures, journals or diaries.

Activity # 6

Goal:	To improve students' ability to make responsible decisions.
Objective:	To understand and appreciate the difference between good touch/bad touch and appropriate times to say "no".
Group:	4-6
Time:	30 minutes
Materials:	None

Class discussion: What would you do in each of the following situations? Who would you tell first? What would you tell the violator in each situation?

Sally likes her stepfather but since her mother started working nights, Sally's stepfather has started touching her places that make her feel uncomfortable. At first it was just hugs which Sally liked, but now he is touching private parts of her body.

Tom's neighbor asked him if he would like to earn some extra money cleaning out his garage. Tom has known Mr. Smith for several years. Tom and Mr. Smith started to clean out the garage on a very hot day. Mr. Smith suggested they take off their shirts. Tom didn't think that was strange until Mr. Smith started acting funny and touching Tom's body. Tom was confused and didn't know what to do.

One of Pam's teachers is also her basketball coach. Pam never thought anything was wrong when Mr. Brown touched her. He often showed her how to improve her game. Lately his touching has made her feel uncomfortable and he has asked her to stay after everybody has gone home for extra practice.

End class by giving students the following suggestions.

√   **Trust your feelings**--If something (touching, words, actions) makes you feel uncomfortable, uneasy, or afraid it isn't good.

√   **You have a right to say "no"**--Your body is private and you have a right to say "no" when somebody is trying to violate your privacy.

√   **Give children key phrases to use**--I don't want to do that; No, I don't feel like it; No, I don't do that.

√   **Don't keep secrets**--Regardless of what that violator may tell you, don't keep any secrets.

√   **Tell someone that you trust**--Tell a parent, teacher, counselor, principal, social worker, police officer, doctor, nurse or minister.

√   **You are the victim**--Whatever your feelings, molestation and sexual abuse are not your fault.

Activity # 7

Goal: To increase awareness of sexual harassment

Objective: To define and understand sexual harassment.

Group: Grades 4-6

Time: 30-45 minutes

Materials: Pencil and paper

Divide the students into groups of 3-6. Make sure that each group has a mix of boys and girls. Appoint one person in the group to be the recorder and one person to be the reporter. Ask the students to write down what they think sexual harassment is, list some behaviors that they think constitute sexual harassment, and note incidents of sexual harassment they've seen happen in the school.

Give the group 15 minutes to come to a consensus. Have each group report and write the results on the board.

Are there any similarities? Think about how you should treat one another (with dignity and respect).

Remind the students that sexual harassment is illegal and the consequences of such action is serious. There may be disagreements, but define sexual harassment as any unwelcome behavior of a sexual nature. If they see sexual harassment, what should be done, who should they report it to?

Activity # 8

Goal: To increase awareness of sexual harassment

Objective: Define and understand sexual harassment.

Group: Grades 4-6

Time: 30-45 minutes

Materials: Newspaper articles

Ask the students to start collecting magazine or newspaper articles about sexual harassment in the workplace or in schools. Give students about a week to gather the articles. Here are some examples of newspaper articles and possible discussion questions:

Katherine Lyle, a former student at Central High School in Duluth, MN received a $15,000 settlement in September of 1991 for "alleged mental anguish and suffering." The award came after an investigation by the state office of civil rights found that the district had failed to act appropriately after sexually offensive graffiti about Katy appeared in a boys' bathroom at the school in 1987 and was not removed despite repeated requests from the Lyles.
                                                  --Education Week 2-10-93

Cheltzie Hentz of Eden Prairie, MN a first grade student came home each day and complained that boys on the bus used "naughty language" and called her obscene names. The behavior was reported to the administration, but the profanity, references to specific body parts, and a suggestion that Cheltzie perform a sexual act on her father continued.
                                                  --Los Angeles Times 12-3-92

Questions: What would you do if this happened to you? How would it make you feel? Do you think the incident was sexual harassment? Who would you tell in school if you were having a problem with sexual harassment? If you were the principal, how would you solve the problem? How would you define sexual harassment? Do you think sexual harassment should be illegal? What other behaviors might be considered sexual harassment?

Bibliography for 4-6 Curriculum

The Big Brag, by Dr. Seuss, in a collection of stories **Six by Seuss,** (1991), Random House.

Molly's Pilgrim, (1983), by Barbara Cohen, Lothrop, Lee and Shepard Books.

My Way Sally, (1988), by Mindy Bingham and Penelope Colville Paine, Advocacy Press, P.O. Box 236, Dept. A, Santa Barbara, CA 93102.

The Sneetches, (1961), by Dr. Seuss, Random House

Chapter Ten

Curriculum For Grades 7-12

Goals:

    1.   To increase awareness of sexual harassment.

Objectives:

    1.   To understand that people have different perceptions of sexual harassment.

    2.   To distinguish between compliments, flirting and sexual harassment.

    3.   To demonstrate how gender bias in the classroom leads to sexual harassment.

    4.   To define and give examples of the hostile work environment.

    5.   To define and understand the three categories of sexual harassment.

    6.   To demonstrate how sexual harassment escalates through elementary and high school and extends to the workplace.

    7.   Evaluation of student's knowledge about sexual harassment.

Activity # 1

Goal: To increase awareness of sexual harassment

Objective: To understand that people have different perceptions of sexual harassment.

Group: Grades 7-12

Time: 30-45 minutes

Materials: Paper and pencil

Divide the class into groups of 3-6 with special attention that each group has a mix of boys and girls. Appoint a student in each group to record the ideas. Have the students write down their ideas about what sexual harassment is. Allow 10-15 minutes for group discussion. When the groups have finished compile the ideas on the board and discuss them. Clarify what sexual harassment review the list again to see if the student's ideas change.

The teacher should review Chapter One. Definitions of sexual harassment and the three types of harassment: *Quid Pro Quo*, Sexual Favoritism and Hostile Educational Environment.

Activity # 2

Goal:	To increase awareness of sexual harassment
Objective:	To distinguish between compliments, flirting, and sexual harassment.
Group:	Grades 7-12
Time:	30-45 minutes
Materials:	Activity sheet and pencil

There are differences among compliments, flirting, and sexual harassment. The difficulty in defining the differences is compounded because males and females often perceive behaviors differently. This activity is designed to stimulate thought and communication between the sexes on the differences between compliments, flirting, and sexual harassment.

Divide into small groups of 3-6 students. Have each group place the number of the phrase on the activity sheet under the category the group decides is most appropriate.

Phrases
1. You look nice in that suit.
2. I really like that perfume you're wearing.
3. You have great looking legs.
4. The dress you are wearing really shows off your great looking legs.
5. You would get better grades if you would be a little nicer to Mr. Nelson.
6. The perfume you're wearing really turns me on.
7. You did a great job organizing the files.
8. She has the sexiest voice when she is talking on the phone.
9. If Jane can't come up with the right answer, I'm sure the boys can.
10. You don't have enough curves for me to grade on the curve.
11. I told you twice before that I don't want to go out with you.
12. Would you like to study together tonight?
13. Whenever I go to class you're always staring and laughing at me.

14.   Last week you started pinching me and daring the other guys to grab me or touch me.
15.   You did a great job on that research paper you handed in on Friday.
16.   I can help you with that research paper if you want to stay after class.
17.   You're failing this class. Why don't you come over to my house tonight so we can work on improving your grades? I'll be alone.
18.   I know I've asked you before, but would you like to go out Saturday night? You said you were busy last time.
19.   In shop class you're always messing with my projects and I end up with a poor grade.
20.   This is the best way for me to explain wants and needs in economics: If I was a teenage boy, I might want Jennifer, but I might not need her.

Questions

√   Do all the phrases fit under a specific category?
√   Do you regard some of the statements as just "teasing" or "boys will be boys" statements?
√   If you place a phrase under flirting, what would make the phrase sexual harassment?
√   Would some of the phrases fit better under discrimination of males and females?
√   Can the discrimination between males and females lead to sexual harassment? Could the behavior escalate into sexual harassment?
√   Did the male-female composition of your group play a significant part in where some statements were placed?

Discussion

The questions may lead in many different directions. There may be disagreement on what is sexual harassment and what is not. Sexual harassment is any unwelcome behavior of a sexual nature. Perceptions are often different between male and female. Sometimes the same gender cannot agree on what is unwelcome behavior, but the person being harassed knows when the line has been crossed. It is that person's responsibility to inform the harasser of the inappropriate behavior and the harasser to stop the behavior without retaliation. Discuss the difference between flirting and sexual harassment. Flirting is two-way, feels good, is reciprocal, wanted behavior by both parties. The purpose of flirting to develop a romantic relationship. Sexual harassment is one-way, one-sided, hurts and makes the victim uncomfortable, is unwanted and unwelcome. The purpose of sexual harassment is to embarrass and humiliate the victim.

Activity Sheet

Compliment	Flirting	Sexual Harassment

Activity # 3

Goal: To increase awareness of sexual harassment

Objective: To demonstrate how gender bias in the classroom leads to sexual harassment.

Group: Grades 7-12

Time: 20-30 minutes

Materials: None

Female students experience gender bias in the classroom as soon as they enter school for the first time. Do the behaviors towards female students from elementary through high school lead to sexual harassment in the workplace? Have the students examine the following scenarios and determine the commonalities.

Elementary School

A second grade teacher is working with a group of seven children. There are 5 girls and 2 boys in the reading group. During the 30-minute questioning/discussion period, not one girl was allowed to answer a question without a boy blurting out the answer before the girl was asked to answer. The girls dutifully raised their hands when questions were asked. The boys raised their hands occasionally, but they always waved or jumped up and down to get the teacher's attention.

High School

A trigonometry class is 75 percent male. During class the female students rarely raise their hands, give fewer correct answers, and are not called on as frequently as the male students.

Workplace

A female has worked as a secretary for fifteen years at a company that sells construction equipment. She has learned the business and knows as much about construction equipment as the male employees but makes about one-third less salary than the men. Her boss has so much confidence in her ability that when he is gone he relies upon her to conduct business in his absence. Although she has never asked for a management position, her boss has never considered her for the job. She is often asked to train the new male employees for a higher-paying position that she is equally qualified to do. While this creates doubts in her mind about her ability to do the work, a more pervasive situation occurs. The men constantly tell suggestive jokes, and send graphic sexual memos to one another on the computer. She never says anything to her boss, hoping that someday she will be considered a team player and get a management position.

Questions

√   Which behaviors, if any, do you consider sexual harassment?

√   What can be done on the elementary level to ensure that girls are getting equal treatment? High school level? In the workplace?

√   If the girls were getting equal treatment at the elementary level, would it change how they handle situations in high school and the workplace?

√   Would the boys' behavior toward their teachers and female coworkers change if they encountered equality in the classroom at all levels of their education?

Activity # 4

Goal: To increase awareness of sexual harassment

Objective: To define and give examples of the hostile work environment in the elementary, high school and workplace.

Group: Grades 7-12

Time: 20-30 minutes

Materials: None

School personnel often are not aware that sexual harassment exists in schools. While inappropriate behavior in the workplace is called sexual harassment, the same behavior at the elementary or high school level is not recognized as sexual harassment because educators are under the mistaken impression that students don't understand sexual themes. This activity will help increase the awareness of inappropriate and appropriate behaviors.

Elementary
A first-grade female student rides the bus everyday to school. Each day a boy in the third grade is using inappropriate language that is graphic and sexual. At one point the boy tells the girl that he is going to " 'F' her in her mouth". The girl reports the behavior several times to the bus driver and the principal.

High School
A senior female student finds out that sexually offensive graffiti on the boys' rest room wall makes a reference to her. She reports it to the counselor and principal, but they tell her that it shouldn't bother her because it is in the boys' rest room not the girls'. She doesn't have to look at it everyday. The principal doesn't want to draw attention to the graffiti because he thinks it will encourage the boys to write more.

Workplace
A female police officer is subjected to lewd remarks, staring, and sexually offensive material left on her desk by fellow police officers. One coworker makes a habit of drinking his coffee out of a mug that is in the shape of a breast. She tries to ignore the behavior, but the situation escalates. When she discusses the situation with her

supervisor, she is told that they are only teasing and if she goes along with it and tease them back they will stop.

Questions

√   Which behaviors, if any, do you consider sexual harassment?

√   Can anything be done to stop the behavior on the bus? Is it the school's responsibility to stop sexual harassment on the bus even though it isn't on school property?

√   Is the graffiti on the rest room wall a serious problem, after all the female student involved never sees the boys' bathroom. She is only basing her complaints on what somebody has told her.

√   Are lewd remarks, staring, and sexually offensive material considered sexual harassment? What is the purpose of having sexually offensive material at school or in the workplace?

√   Is it all right to have sexually suggestive of material at your own desk in your own space?

Activity # 5

Goal: To increase awareness of sexual harassment

Objective: Define and understand the three categories of
                     sexual harassment.

Group: Grades 7-12

Time: 30-45 minutes

Materials: Newspaper articles

   This activity can be done in a large group discussion or
students can be divided into groups of 3-6 with attention given to
equal numbers of males and females in the groups.

Example newspaper articles

In the presence of her teacher and a roomful of classmates, Ms.
Mennone says a male peer grabbed her hair, legs, breasts, and
buttocks nearly every day. He repeatedly made remarks about her
breasts and told her that he was going to rape her. He allegedly
continued the behavior after her complaint.
                              ---Education Week 2-10-93

Tawnya Brawdy, a student at Kenilworth Junior High in northern
California, filed a suit against the school district alleging that when
boys "mooed" and commented on her breasts, the school district did
not take appropriate action to stop the behavior. The out of court
settlement was $20,000.
                              --Education Week 2-10-93

   How would you handle each situation if you were the
student? Would you report the behavior to another adult? To which
adult would you report the behavior? If the behavior did not change,
what would you do next? If you were the principal in charge of the
school, how would you handle student complaints? Is each case an
example of sexual harassment?

Activity # 6

Goal: To increase awareness of sexual harassment

Objective: To demonstrate how sexual harassment escalates through elementary and high school to the workplace.

Group: Grades 7-12

Time: 20-30 minutes

Materials: None

Is sexually harassing behavior at the elementary school level taken as seriously as in high school or the workplace? Have the students examine the following scenarios and determine the commonalities.

Elementary School
A second-grade boy was constantly touching a girl in his class. The behaviors included touching her hair, and shoving and pushing her. Most the incidents occurred at recess, but in the classroom he found ways to be around her desk. The girl is intimidated by the behavior. The teacher tells the girl to ignore him.

High School
Boys gather in the hallway between classes and laugh at the girls who walk by. The situation escalates right before the bell rings as the boys close in on the girls and make it impossible for the girls to walk down the hallway without being physically being touched. The teachers observing the behavior dismiss it as "typical high school " or "boys will be boys" behavior.

Workplace

A female administrator was told when she was hired never to go in the bus barn and to have a male administrator or the maintenance men pick up the supplies that were stored there. One day she couldn't locate any help and decided to pick up a box of paper herself. When she entered the bus barn, she found pornographic pictures displayed all around the area. When she reported the pictures to the superintendent, he said, "You were told not to go into the bus barn. We never had this problem until we hired a female administrator."

Questions

√   Which behaviors, if any, do you consider sexual harassment?

√   Would you consider any of the behaviors described in the three situations to be just teasing or typical male behavior?

√   If behaviors were changed at the elementary and high school levels would that affect how women are treated in the workplace?

√   Does allowing employees to display pornographic pictures on school property, permit inappropriate sexual behaviors in students to be overlooked?

√   What has your school district established as standards for behavior?

Activity # 7

Goal: To increase awareness of sexual harassment

Objective: To demonstrate how sexual harassment escalates through elementary and high school to the workplace.

Group: Grades 7-12

Time: 20-30 minutes

Materials: None

Is sexually harassing behavior at the elementary school level taken as seriously as it is in high school or the workplace? Have the students examine the following scenarios and determine the commonalities.

Elementary School
The female principal gets a short haircut. A sixth grade student named Jay runs his fingers up through the back of the principal's hair while she is talking to another student in the lunchroom. She turns around and Jay says, "Do you like it?" She asks him, "Like what?" Jay says, "Your new hair cut." The principal is so stunned by his action that she can't think of anything to say but "yes".

High School
John, a high school freshman, is Jay's brother. One day on the bus he grabs a high school girl's breast. The girl tells the bus driver who is also her mother but begs her not to turn in a disciplinary report to the principal about the incident.

Workplace
Jake, the father of Jay and John, works at an appliance store. During his lunch break he goes to a local cafe to eat. He knows many of the regulars at the cafe including the waitresses. Although Jake has never touched any of the waitresses, they hate to see him come into the cafe. Every word out of Jake's mouth is sexual innuendo or taunting.

Questions

√ Which behaviors, if any do you consider sexual harassment?

√   Would you consider any behavior in the three situations to be just teasing, or typical male behavior?

√   Why do you think the girl didn't want her mother to report the incident?

√   If behaviors were changed at the elementary and high school level, would that have any affect on how women are treated in the workplace?

√   Does Jay's and John's behavior have anything to do with their father's behavior?

√   Can anything be done to change Jay's and John's behavior now so that they become more responsible adults?

Activity # 8

Goal: To increase awareness of sexual harassment

Objective: To demonstrate how sexual harassment escalates through elementary and high school to the workplace.

Group: Grades 7-12

Time: 20-30 minutes

Materials: None

Is sexually harassing behavior at the elementary school level taken as seriously as it is in high school or the workplace? Have the students examine the following scenarios and determine the commonalities.

Elementary School

After a day at school, Allison, a first grader tells her father about a game they played called "dog". Allison explained that it is lots of fun. The girls stand next to one of the boys. The boy throws a stick across the playground and the girls race each other to fetch the stick. The girl that gets the stick first brings it back to the boy. The girls never get an opportunity to throw the stick.

High School

On a slave day each girl is assigned to a boy. The girl wears a dog collar and has a sign hanging around their neck that indicates which boy she belongs to. The girl is required to crawl around on her hands and knees being a slave to the boy. A reverse situation of "slave day" never occurs.

Workplace

At a dog food company a group of men yell and hoot at women on a daily basis. The men start "barking" at Connie and call her a "dog" whenever she enters their work area. She tries ignoring the behavior, but the situation continues to escalate. The men now bark and throw dog food at her when she walks through the warehouse.

Questions

√   Which behaviors, if any, do you consider sexual harassment?

√   Would you consider any behavior in the three situations to be just teasing or having a good time?

√   If behaviors were changed at the elementary and high school level, would that have any affect on how women are treated later on in the workplace?

Activity # 9

Goal: To increase awareness of sexual harassment

Objective: To define and understand the three categories of sexual harassment.

Group: Grades 7-12

Time: 30-45 minutes

Materials: Video tape *Sexual Harassment: What Is It And Why Should I Care?*

Synopsis

Sexual Harassment: What Is It And Why Should I Care? is an entertaining and informative video that explains and discusses sexual harassment in terms everyone can understand. A series of very effective vignettes presents each type of sexual harassment, including student-to-student harassment.

Use the video tape to show the three categories of sexual harassment. Ask the following questions after showing the opening vignette where a female student is being harassed by her teacher.

Questions

√   Do you think sexual harassment has occurred in this situation? Why or why not?

√   Were the teacher's comments appropriate? Why or why not?

√   Was the way the teacher touched the student appropriate? Why or why not? Would you allow a teacher to touch you in that manner? How would it make you feel?

√   What should the female student do? What would you do if you were in a similar situation?

√   If the female student tried to ignore the behavior, what would happen?

Explain the term *Quid Pro Quo* and give examples drawn from the school setting and workplace. Use the examples and explanations in Chapter Four of this book.

Activity # 10

Goal: To increase awareness of sexual harassment

Objective: To define and understand the three categories
                   of sexual harassment.

Group: Grades 7-12

Time: 30-45 minutes

Materials: *Video tape Sexual Harassment: What Is It
                   And Why Should I Care?*

Synopsis

Sexual Harassment: What Is It And Why Should I Care? is
an entertaining and informative video that explains and discusses
sexual harassment in terms everyone can understand. A series of
very effective vignettes presents each type of sexual harassment,
including student-to-student harassment.

The second vignette in the video tape shows Dr. Shoop on talk show
taking a call from a female who works in a warehouse. Ask the
following questions after watching the vignette.

Questions

√   Do you think sexual harassment has occurred in this
       situation? Why or why not?

√   Discuss any concerns about how men and women
       perceive the same behavior in very different
       ways.

√   What were some of the things that made the female employee feel uncomfortable? Have you seen similar things at school? How do they make you feel?

Additional Activity
Explain the term hostile work environment and hostile educational environment. Examples and explanations are found in Chapter Four. Have the students make a list of things at school that would be considered to be a hostile educational environment.

Activity # 11

Goal: To increase awareness of sexual harassment

Objective: To define and understand the three categories of sexual harassment.

Group: Grades 7-12

Time: 30-45 minutes

Materials: Video tape *Sexual Harassment: What Is It And Why Should I Care?*

Synopsis

Sexual Harassment: What Is It And Why Should I Care? is an entertaining and informative video that explains and discusses sexual harassment in terms everyone can understand. A series of very effective vignettes presents each of the types of sexual harassment, including student-to-student harassment.

The third vignette in the video tape shows a female administrator talking with a male teacher. Two other male teachers witness the encounter. After viewing the vignette, stop the tape and ask the following questions.

Questions

√ Do you think sexual harassment has occurred in this situation? Why or why not?

√ Do you think the two males witnessing the encounter were being sexually harassed? Why or why not?

√ Should the incident be reported? Why or why not?

√ If left alone, what is the likely outcome of this situation?

√ What can be done now to remedy the situation?

Explain the term sexual favoritism. Examples and explanations are found in Chapter Four.

Activity # 12

Goal: To increase awareness of sexual harassment

Objective: To define and understand the three categories
                   of sexual harassment.

Group: Grades 7-12

Time: 30-45 minutes

Materials: Video tape Sexual Harassment: What Is It
                   And Why Should I Care?

Synopsis

   Sexual Harassment: What Is It And Why Should I Care? is
an entertaining and informative video that explains and discusses
sexual harassment in terms everyone can understand. A series of
very effective vignettes presents each of the types of sexual
harassment, including student-to-student harassment.

The fourth, fifth, and sixth vignettes in the video tape occur between
a man and subordinate woman in an office setting. The man is
commenting on the woman's suit. After the vignette, stop the tape
and ask the following questions.

Questions

   √   Do you think sexual harassment has occurred in this
        situation? Why or why not?

   √   Discuss any concerns about friendly personal
        relations in the workplace or at school.

   √   Were the comments appropriate for the workplace?
        Which one(s)?

   √   Discuss any concerns about how men and women
        perceive the same behavior in very different
        ways.

Additional Activity

Explain the term hostile work environment and hostile educational environment. Examples and explanations are found in Chapter Four. Have the students make a list of examples of things that are in your own school that would be considered to be a hostile educational environment.

Activity # 13

Goal: To increase awareness of sexual harassment

Objective: To define and understand the three categories
                    of sexual harassment.

Group: Grades 7-12

Time: 30-45 minutes

Materials: Video tape *Sexual Harassment: What Is It
                    And Why Should I Care?*

Synopsis
      Sexual Harassment: What Is It And Why Should I Care? is
an entertaining and informative video that explains and discusses
sexual harassment in terms everyone can understand. A series of
very effective vignettes presents each of the types of sexual
harassment, including student-to-student harassment.

The next vignette in the video tape occurs in a warehouse where a
female worker is confronted by a frontal nude type centerfold. After
the vignette, stop the tape and ask the following questions.

Questions

√   Do you think sexual harassment has occurred in this
       situation? Why or why not?

√   Nothing of a sexual nature was ever said and the
       female was never touched. Is this sexual
       harassment?

√   If the centerfold picture was never seen by females,
       would it still be appropriate in the workplace? What
       about in a school locker?

√   Are you violating the male employee's free speech
       rights if you ask him to take the pin-up calendar or
       centerfold down?

√   What category of sexual harassment is this?

Additional Activity

Explain the term hostile work environment and hostile educational environment. Examples and explanations are found in Chapter Four. Have the students make a list of examples of things that are in your own school that would be considered to be a hostile educational environment.

Activity # 14

Goal: To increase awareness of sexual harassment

Objective: To define and understand the three categories
                           of sexual harassment.

Group: Grades 7-12

Time: 30-45 minutes

Materials: *Video tape Sexual Harassment: What Is It
                           And Why Should I Care?*

Synopsis

Sexual Harassment: What Is It And Why Should I Care? is
an entertaining and informative video that explains and discusses
sexual harassment in terms everyone can understand. A series of
very effective vignettes presents each of the types of sexual
harassment, including student-to-student harassment.

The next vignette in the video tape is a series of three vignettes
showing interactions between a male and female student. After the
vignette, stop the tape and ask the following questions.

Questions

√   Do you think sexual harassment has occurred in this
          situation? Why or why not?

√   At what point do you think the interaction changed
          from appropriate behavior to inappropriate behavior?

√   What could the female student have done differently?

√   If left alone, what is the likely outcome of this
          situation?

√   What can be done now to remedy the situation?

√   How would you report such an incident? To Whom
          would you report it?

Review sexual harassment policies and procedures with students.

Activity # 15

Goal:	To increase awareness of sexual harassment
Objective:	Define and understand the three categories of sexual harassment.
Group:	Grades 7-12
Time:	30-45 minutes
Materials:	*Video tape Sexual Harassment: What Is It And Why Should I Care?*

Synopsis

Sexual Harassment: What Is It And Why Should I Care? is an entertaining and informative video that explains and discusses sexual harassment in terms everyone can understand. A series of very effective vignettes presents each of the types of sexual harassment, including student-to-student harassment.

The final vignette in the video tape takes place in the stairwell of a secondary school. The male students have a tradition of "handing out" and hassling female students as they walk to and from class. After the vignette, stop the tape and ask the following questions.

Questions

√ Do you think sexual harassment has occurred in this situation? Why or why not?

√ Can the school district be held liable for student to student sexual harassment?

√ Should this incident be reported? How could this situation be prevented? How should the incident be reported?

√ If left alone, what is the likely outcome of this situation?

√   What can be done now to remedy the situation?

√   Do incidents like this happen in your school? How do you handle them?

√   How would you handle this situation in the workplace? To whom would you report the incident?

Activity # 16

Goal: To increase awareness of sexual harassment

Objective: To assess the current knowledge of sexual harassment.

Group: Grades 7-12

Time: 30-45 minutes

Materials: Questionnaire and pencil

There are different levels of understanding of sexual harassment. This questionnaire will identify areas of confusion or differences of perception. The answer sheet will provide the instructor with explanations useful in a discussion of sexual harassment.

Questionnaire on Sexual Harassment

1. T   F   Sexual harassment is a trivial problem involving limited numbers of students.

2. T   F   Women are the only victims of sexual harassment.

3. T   F   Only young and attractive women are subjected to sexual harassment.

4. T   F   Sexual harassment is usually an isolated incident that will not be repeated.

5. T   F   Ignoring the harasser will make the behavior stop.

6. T   F   Females dress in a way that invites sexual harassment.

7. T   F   Treating females as equals at school and making the organization free of harassment will result in female students receiving preferential treatment.

8. T   F   Sexual harassment is illegal under Title VII of the Civil Rights Act.

9.   T   F   Continued sexual harassment can lead to health problems similar to those in other stressful situations.

10. T   F   Sexual harassment is a problem for students in school.

11. T   F   Sexual harassment is only committed by people in authority such as teachers or principals.

12. T   F   Displaying material that is sexually suggestive (pornographic photos, jokes or drawings) is sexual harassment.

13. T   F   To be defined as sexual harassment both the victim and the harasser must consider the behavior unwanted or unwelcome.

14. T   F   Men can harass other men and women can harass other women.

15. T   F   Ten percent of the sexual harassment charges filed with the EEOC are filed by men.

16. T   F   Preferential treatment of one student or teacher who is having an affair with a teacher or administrator is sexual harassment.

17. T   F   A student can no longer compliment a fellow student without the fear of being charged with sexual harassment.

18.   T   F   A school district can be held liable for ignoring sexual harassment by all district employees, students and non-employees.

19.   T   F   Retaliation for reporting sexual harassment in the form of grades, job demotion, transfer or firing is illegal.

20.   T   F   A hostile educational environment exists in a school if the educational environment is negatively affected.

Answers

1. **False.** Public opinion polls indicate that over 70 percent of female students are sexually harassed at school.

2. **False.** Ninety percent of the sexual harassment charges each year are filed by women according to the Equal Employment Opportunity Commission.

3. **False.** Seventy percent of the respondents to a survey by the American Association of University Women have been sexually harassed in school. A 1980 Merit Board survey showed that a diversity of women (regardless of appearance, age, race, marital status, occupation, or socio-economic class) were sexually harassed. Sexual harassment is not an expression of attraction, but an expression of power over another person and/or an assertion of hostility.

4. **False.** Quite often harassers bother more than one person, and the incidents reoccur over an extended period of time.

5. **False.** It is not uncommon for a victim of sexual harassment to ignore the offensive behavior. In fact it is estimated that 46 percent of victims of harassment try this strategy. However, only one of four women who tried to ignore or avoid her harasser was successful in getting the harasser to stop. Approximately one-third of the harassers who were told to stop did so. Choosing to ignore the behavior will not make it clear to the harasser that the behavior is inappropriate. Ignoring harassment may allow the harasser think that his behavior is acceptable.

6. **False.** It is the responsibility of the school administration to tell teachers or students if their clothes are inappropriate for school. However, regardless of how a person is dressed, no teacher or student has the right to act inappropriately.

7. **False.** Although 90 percent of the reported incidents of sexual harassment are made by women, most men do not condone inappropriate behavior. Many men are just as offended and outraged by sexual harassment

as are women. Eliminating sexual harassment does not give women an unfair advantage. On the contrary, it ensures that all employees will be treated fairly.

8. **True.** Sexual harassment is a form or subset of sexual discrimination and is therefore prohibited by Title IX.

9. **True.** Sexual harassment can lead to health problems that are similar to health problems created by stress, headaches, chronic fatigue, nausea, frequent colds, urinary tract infections, and sleep and appetite disorders.

10. **True.** A significant number of high school female students report sexual harassment. The same problems that occur for adults in the workplace are very similar for students. This behavior has a significant impact on their self-esteem and emotional well being as well as resulting in a denial of equal educational opportunity.

11. **False.** People in authority are not the only ones that commit sexual harassment. Other students can make the school intolerable for their peers.

12. **True.** Sexually oriented conduct or any sexually oriented atmosphere that is intimidating or offensive can be a hostile educational environment. Displaying material that is sexually suggestive such, following a person, leering at a person's body, writing unwanted letters, or giving unwanted gifts, are all examples of occurrences in a hostile educational environment.

13. **False.** It is the victim's perspective and not the harasser's that matters in sexual harassment charges.

14. **True.** Approximately ten percent of the sexual harassment charges filed each year with the Equal Employment Opportunity Commission are filed by men. Most of the complaints filed are by women that are harassed by men, but men can be harassed by females and there is also same-gender sexual harassment.

15. **True.** Same answer as in number 14.

16. **True.** Sexual favoritism occurs when a student receives preferential treatment over another student as a result of submission to a teacher's sexual advances.

17. **False.** There is nothing in the law or in any court decision that restricts normal, polite conversation. Teachers and students do not need to worry about being friendly. As long as the behavior is not unwanted, it is not sexual harassment.

18. **True.** The U.S. Supreme Court ruled that students who claim they were sexually harassed may seek monetary damages in addition to other remedies when they sue the school and or school officials. A school district can be sued, as can as any workplace environment, for sexual harassment.

19. **True.** Retaliation for reporting sexual harassment is illegal.

20. **True.** Same answer as in number 12.

Resources for 9-12 Curriculum

Sexual Harassment: What Is It And Why Should I Care?, (1993), Quality Work Environments, P.O. Box 1945, Manhattan, KS 66502

Appendixes

Appendix A
Sample Policies, Forms and Notices

Sample State Statute Against Sexual Harassment

Minnesota Human Rights Act, Minn. Stat. §§363.01-.14 (West 1966 & Supp. 1992)

127.455 MODEL POLICY

The commissioner of education shall maintain and make available to school boards a model sexual harassment and violence policy. The model policy shall address the requirements of section 127.46.

Each school board shall submit to the commissioner of education a copy of the sexual harassment and sexual violence policy the board has adopted.

127.46   SEXUAL HARASSMENT AND VIOLENCE POLICY (Amended 1992)

Each school board shall adopt a written sexual harassment and sexual violence policy that conforms with sections 363.01 to 363.15. The policy shall apply to pupils, teachers, administrators, and other school personnel, include reporting procedures, and set forth disciplinary actions that will be taken for violation of the policy. Disciplinary actions must conform with collective bargaining agreements and sections 127.27 to 127.39. The policy must be conspicuously posted throughout each school building and included in each school's student handbook on school policies. Each school must develop a process for discussing the school's sexual harassment and violence policy with students and school employees.

(After reviewing the statutes of each state and the District of Columbia, we choose the statute from Minnesota as an example of a comprehensive state statute.)

Sample School District Policy

Sexual Harassment And Sexual Violence Policy

I. General Policy

Sexual harassment is a form of discrimination prohibited by Title VII of the Civil Rights Act of 1964 and Title IX of the Education Amendments of 1972. Sexual harassment is any unwanted attention of a sexual nature. Sexual violence is a physical act of aggression that includes a sexual act or sexual purpose.

(Your School's Name) is committed to maintaining a learning environment that is free from sexual harassment and sexual violence, where all employees and students can work and study together comfortably and productively. The School District prohibits any form of sexual harassment or sexual violence.

It shall be a violation of this policy for any student or employee of **(Your School's Name)** to harass a student or an employee through conduct or communication of a sexual nature as defined by this policy. It shall be a violation of this policy for any student or employee of **(Your School's Name)** to be sexually violent to a student or employee.

The School District will act to investigate all complaints, either formal or informal, verbal or written, of sexual harassment or sexual violence and to discipline any student or employee who sexually harasses or is sexually violent to a student or employee of the School District.

II. Definition of Sexual Harassment and Sexual Violence

Sexual harassment consists of unwelcome sexual advances, requests for sexual favors, sexually motivated physical conduct or other verbal or physical conduct or communication of a sexual nature when:

1. Submission to such conduct is made either explicitly or implicitly a term or condition of an individual's employment, or of obtaining an education; or

2.   Submission to or rejection of that conduct or communication by an individual is used as a factor in decisions affecting that individual's employment or education; or

3.   The conduct or communication has the purpose or effect of substantially or unreasonably interfering with an individual's work employment or education, or creating an intimidating, hostile, or offensive employment or eduction environment.

Examples of prohibited behavior that is sexual in nature and is unsolicited and unwelcome include:

• **Written Contact**--sexually suggestive or obscene letters, notes, invitations, drawings. This also includes computer terminal messages of a sexual nature.

• **Verbal Contact**--sexually suggestive or obscene comments, threats, jokes (including jokes about racial and gender-specific traits), any sexual propositions, comments about an employee's body or sexual characteristics that are used in a negative or embarrassing way.

• **Physical Contact**--any intentional pats, squeezes, touching, pinching, repeatedly brushing up against another's body, assault, blocking movement, or coercing sexual intercourse.

• **Visual Contact**--suggestive looks, leering, or staring at another's body, gesturing, displaying sexually suggestive objects or pictures, cartoons, posters or magazines.

• **Sexual Blackmail**--Sexual behavior to control another employee's work environment is also prohibited--this includes salary, promotions, evaluations and/or better job assignments or grades.

Every effort will be made to eliminate sexual harassment by non-employees including parents, suppliers, and other visitors to the school.

III. Reporting Procedures

Any person who believes he or she has been the victim of sexual harassment by a student or an employee of the School District, or any person with knowledge or belief of conduct which may constitute sexual harassment or sexual violence, should report the alleged acts immediately to an appropriate School District official as designated by this policy. The School District encourages the reporting party or complainant to make his or her report in writing.

A.   **In Each School Building.** The building principal is the person responsible for receiving oral or written reports of sexual harassment or sexual violence at the building level. Upon receipt of a report, the principal must notify the Manager of Human Resources immediately without screening or investigating the report. A written report will be forwarded simultaneously to the Manager of Human Resources. If the report is given verbally, the principal shall reduce it to written form within 24 hours and forward it to the Manager of Human Resources. Failure to forward any sexual harassment or sexual violence report or complaint as provided herein will result in disciplinary action. If the complaint involves the building principal the complaint shall be filed directly with the Manager of Human Resources.

B.   **District-Wide.** The School Board hereby designates the Manager of Human Resources to receive reports or complaints of sexual harassment and sexual violence from any individual, employee or victim of sexual harassment or sexual violence and also from the building principals as outlined above. If the complaint involves the Manager of Human Resources, the complaint shall be filed directly with the Superintendent. If the complaint involves the Superintendent, the complaint shall be filed with the Manager of Human Resources, who shall report the complaint to the Chair of the School Board.

The School District shall conspicuously post the name of the Manager of Human Resources, including a mailing address and telephone number.

C.   Submission of a complaint or report of sexual harassment or sexual violence will not affect the individual's future employment, grades, or work assignments.

D.   Use of written complaints is not mandatory. The School District will respect the confidentiality of the complainant and the individual(s) against whom the complaint is filed, as much as possible, consistent with the School District's legal obligations and the necessity to investigate allegations of sexual harassment and sexual violence and take disciplinary action when the conduct has occurred.

IV. Investigation and Recommendation

By authority of the School District, the Manager of Human Resources, upon receipt of a report or complaint alleging sexual harassment or sexual violence, shall immediately authorize an investigation. This investigation may be conducted by School District officials or by a third party designated by the School District. The investigating party shall provide a written report of the status of the investigation within 10 working days to the Superintendent of Schools and the Manager of Human Resources.

In determining whether the alleged conduct constitutes sexual harassment or sexual violence, the School District should consider the surrounding circumstances, the nature of the sexual advances, relationships between parties involved, and the context in which the alleged incidents occurred. Whether a particular action or incident constitutes sexual harassment or sexual violence requires a determination based on all the facts and the surrounding circumstances.

The investigation may consist of personal interviews with the complainant, the individual(s) against whom the complaint is filed, and others who have knowledge of the alleged incident(s) or circumstances giving rise to the complaint. The investigation may also consist of any other methods and documents deemed pertinent by the investigator.

In addition, the School District may take immediate steps, at its discretion, to protect the complainant, students, and employees pending the completion of an investigation of alleged sexual harassment or sexual violence.

The Manager of Human Resources shall make a report to the Superintendent upon completion of the investigation.

V. School District Action

A.   Upon receipt of a recommendation that the complaint is valid, the District will take such action, as appropriate, based on the results of the investigation.

B.   The result of the investigation of each complaint filed under these procedures will be reported in writing to the complainant by the School District. The report will document any disciplinary action taken as a result of the complaint.

VI. Reprisal

The School District will discipline any individual who retaliates against any person who reports alleged sexual harassment or sexual violence or retaliates against any person who testifies, assists, or participates in an investigation proceeding or hearing relating to a sexual harassment or sexual violence complaint. Retaliation includes, but is not limited to, any form of intimidation, reprisal, or harassment.

VII. Right to Alternative Complaint Procedures

These procedures do not deny the right of any individual to pursue other avenues of recourse which may include filing charges with the State Department of Human Rights, initiating civil action, or seeking redress under state criminal statutes and or federal law.

VIII. Sexual Harassment or Sexual Violence as Sexual Abuse

(Under certain circumstances, sexual harassment or sexual violence may constitute sexual abuse under state statutes. In such situations School Districts shall comply with their state reporting procedures.) Nothing in this policy will prohibit the School District from taking immediate action to protect victims of alleged sexual abuse.

IX. Discipline

Any School District action taken pursuant to this policy will be consistent with requirements of applicable collective bargaining agreements, State and District policies. The School District will take such disciplinary action it deems necessary and appropriate, including warning, suspension or immediate discharge, or expulsion, in the case of a student, to end sexual harassment and sexual violence and prevent its recurrence.

X . Training

Training is the key in establishing a prevention plan for sexual harassment. Yearly training sessions for all employees and students concerning rights and legal options will be established. New employee orientation sessions will include training in sexual harassment. Administrators and teachers will be trained in how to keep the school free from sexual harassment and how to handle sexual harassment complaints.

After reviewing scores of school district sexual harassment policies, we choose the policy from South Washington County Schools, Cottage Grove, Minnesota as the basis for our model policy. Although we have modified their policy by adding material from other policies, it is still interesting to compare this policy to the Minnesota Statute on Sexual Harassment. The South Washington County Schools policy was revised in November of 1990.

Sample Sexual Harassment Notice

"Your School District's Name"

PROHIBITS

Sexual Harassment

Sexual Harassment
is a form of discrimination
prohibited by Title IX of the Education Amendments
of 1972.

Sexual harassment is any unwanted
attention of a sexual nature.

Incidents of sexual harassment
should be reported to **"NAME OF PERSON."**
To report incidents, call:

000-0000

"Your School's Name"

Sample Letter to Harasser

Date

John Doe
XYZ School
City, State   00000

Mr. Doe:

On November 1, 1993 you asked me out and made comments about my body and clothing saying "you would look better in short skirts." I told you that I was not interested in a social relationship and I didn't like your comments about my clothes or body.

Today as I passed you in the hallway, you brushed up against me and asked me to meet you after school. When I turned and walked away you patted me on the buttocks. This was a very embarrassing situation because several other students observed this behavior.

I have no interest in a social relationship and your persistent comments about my clothing, my body, touching me, and meeting you socially are very upsetting to me. I do not want any personal relationship with you.

I have attached our school's policy on sexual harassment. The behavior that I have described is a clear violation of our policy and is also illegal under federal law.

If you continue in this behavior, I will take action at once by taking this letter with me when I discuss this matter with the principal.

Sincerely,

Sexual Harassment Complaint Form

Name:_____

Date:_____

Department:_____

Who was responsible for the
harassment?_____

Describe the sexual harassment.

_____

_____

_____

_____

Date, time, and place the harassment occurred.

_____

_____

Were there other employees or students involved with the
harassment?

_____

_____

If so, who was responsible and describe their involvement.

_____

_____

_____

List any witnesses to the harassment.

_____

_____

What was your reaction to the harassment?

_____

_____

Describe any subsequent incidents.

_____

_____

_____

_____

Signature of Complainant

Administrative Follow-up Form

Date of investigation
_____

What action was taken
_____
_____
_____
_____

Date of follow-up conference
_____

Results of the conference
_____
_____
_____
_____

Date of final report _____

Date copy sent to employee/student_____

_____

Signature of Administrator

Appendix B
A Summary of EEOC Guidelines

SEC. 1604.11 Sexual Harassment

(a) Harassment on the basis of sex is a violation of Sec. 703 of Title VII. Unwelcome sexual advances, requests for sexual favors, and other verbal or physical conduct of a sexual nature constitute sexual harassment when (1) submission to such conduct is made either explicitly or implicitly a term or condition of an individual's employment, (2) submission to or rejection of such conduct by an individual is used as the basis for employment decisions affecting such individual, or (3) such conduct has the purpose or effect of unreasonably interfering with an individual's work performance or creating an intimidating, hostile, or offensive working environment.

(b) In determining whether alleged conduct constitutes sexual harassment, the Commission will look at the record as a whole and the totality of the circumstances, such as the nature of the sexual advances and the context in which the alleged incidents occurred. The determination of the legality of a particular action will be made from the facts, on a case by case basis.

(c) Applying general Title VII principles, an employer, employment agency, joint apprenticeship committee or labor organization (hereinafter collectively referred to as "employer") is responsible for its acts and those of its agents and supervisory employees with respect to sexual harassment regardless of whether the specific acts complained of were authorized or even forbidden by the employer and regardless of whether the employer knew or should have known of this occurrence. The Commission will examine the circumstances of the particular employment relationship and the job functions performed by the individual in determining whether an individual acts in either a supervisory or agency capacity.

(d) With respect to conduct between fellow employees, an employer is responsible for acts of sexual harassment in the workplace where the employer (or its agents or supervisory employees) knows or should have known of the conduct, unless it can show that it took immediate and appropriate corrective action.

(e) An employer may also be responsible for the acts of non-employees, with respect to sexual harassment of employees in the workplace, where the employer (or its agents or supervisory employees) knows or should have known of the conduct and fails to take immediate and appropriate corrective action. In reviewing these cases the Commission will consider the extent of the employer's control and any other legal responsibility which the employer may have with respect to the conduct of such non-employees.

(f) Prevention is the best tool for the elimination of sexual harassment. An employer should take all steps necessary to prevent sexual harassment from occurring, such as affirmatively raising the subject, expressing strong disapproval, developing appropriate sanctions, informing employees of their right to raise, and how to raise, the issue of harassment under Title VII, and developing methods to sensitize all concerned.

(g) Other related practices: Where employment opportunities or benefits are granted because of an individual's submission to the employer's requests for sexual favors, the employer may be held liable for unlawful sex discrimination against other persons who were qualified for but denied that employment opportunity or benefit. [Section 1604.11 reads as last amended by 45 FR 74676, effective November 10, 1980]

Appendix C
Selected Cases In The Legal History of Sexual Harassment

1972

N. Jay Rogers v. EEOC, 454 F.2d 234 (5th Cir. 1971). cert. denied, 406 U.S. 957 (1972).
The hostile work environment theory was first presented in this case. A Spanish surnamed woman charged that her work environment was so heavily polluted with discrimination as to destroy the emotional and psychological stability of all minority group workers. The court acknowledged that an individual's well-being could be undermined by a series of complex and persuasive activities.

Connon v. University of Chicago, 441 U.S. 677 (1972).
In this case the U.S. Supreme Court held that a student had an implied right of action for discrimination under Title IX of the Education Amendments of 1972. Title IX bars discrimination in educational programs that receive federal funds.

1978

Heelan v. Johns-Manville Corp., 451 F. Supp. 1382 (D.Colo. 1978).
An employee who refused to have sex with a supervisor was terminated. The court ruled that an employer can be relieved of liability for harassment by a supervisor only if the employer 1) had a policy of discouraging harassment, 2) the employee failed to present the matter to a publicized grievance board, and 3) the employer failed to rectify the situation.

1981

EEOC v. Sage Realty Corp., 507 F. Supp. 599 (S.D. N.Y. 1981).
A lobby attendant was discharged for refusing to wear a revealing bicentennial uniform. The building management corporation and its cleaning contractor were held jointly liable for sex discrimination in violation of Title VII.

Bundy v. Jackson. 641 F.2d 934 (D.C.Cir. 1981).
Sexual harassment may amount to discrimination even if there is no loss of tangible job benefits. An employer is responsible

for discriminatory acts of its agents or supervisors regardless of whether the employer knew or should have know of the acts, but may negate liability by taking immediate and appropriate corrective action.

1982

Gan v. Kepro Circuit Systems, 28 FEP Cases 639 (E.D. Mo. 1982).
The court ruled that a female employee who regularly used vulgar language, initiated sexually oriented conversations with counselors, asked male employees about their sex lives, and discussed her own marital sexual relations, was not constructively discharged. The court ruled that she had contributed to the distasteful working environment by her own conduct and in fact welcomed the conduct.

1983

Barrnett v. Omaha National Bank, 584 F. Supp. 22 (D.Neb. 1983).
Because of the Bank's remedial response to a female employee's complaint of her male co-worker's inappropriate behavior on a business trip, the claim against the bank failed. The bank launched an investigation within four days. The perpetrator was placed on 90 day probation, warned that future misconduct would result in termination, and was passed by for pay raises for 15 months. A letter reporting the incident was placed in his personnel file. For failing to intervene, another male employee was reprimanded, passed over at least three times for promotions, and denied raises for 18 months. A letter was also placed in his file.

Cummings v. Walsh Construction Co., 561 F. Supp. 872 (S.D. Ga. 1983).
A female employee who rebuffed advances of supervisors was required to perform harsh and unpleasant tasks. Sexual harassment was so widespread that the company had constructive knowledge of it; top level management personnel were involved in the activity, therefore the company was liable for the activity even though the company policy was violated.

Katz v. Dole,700 F. 2d 251, 31 FEP Cases 1521, 1524 (4th Cir. 1983).
In this case the court noted that, since any act of sexual harassment was "an intentional assault on an individual's innermost

privacy," once the plaintiff proves that the harassment took place, "the most difficult legal question will concern the responsibility of the employer for that harassment."

1985

Horn v. Duke Homes, 755 F.2d 599 (7th Cir. 1985).
The corporation was held strictly liable under doctrine of *respondeat superior* where a plant supervisor used his authority to hire and fire employees and to extort sex from female employees in exchange for keeping their jobs.

King v. Palmer, 778 F.2d 878 (D.C. Cir. 1985).
The concept of sexual favoritism as a category of sexual harassment was presented when an employee who established that a sexual relationship between her supervisor and another employee influenced that employee promotion over her was not required to prove the sexual relationship had been consummated.

Boyd v. Hayes Living Health Care Agency, 44 FEP Cases 332 (W.D. Tenn. 1985).
Even though the administrator did not expressly invite her to have a sexual relationship or force one on her, the court ruled that a female employee was sexually harassed by an administrator, when he insisted that she come to his hotel room, offered her wine, tried to get her to look at a sexually explicit movie and magazines, attempted to restrain her departure, and slammed the door in anger when she left.

Harrison v. Reed Rubber Co., 603 F.Supp. 1457 (E.D.Mo. 1985).
A factory line worker was demoted after complaining of her superintendent's open and unwelcome affection for her. Instructions to plant supervisors to stay away from an employee, without directions to cease harassment and without monitoring by the employer, were not enough to preclude employer liability.

Downes v. FAA, 775 F.2d 288 (Fed.Cir. 1985).
Five incidents of sexually offensive conduct in three years did not establish a pattern sufficient to constitute a pervasively hostile environment.

1986

Moylan v. Maries County, 792 F.2d 746 (8th Cir. 1986).
   The Eighth Circuit held that a sexually hostile work environment constituted a violation of Title VII.

Meritor Savings Bank v. Vinson, 447 U.S. 57, (1986).
   The U.S. Supreme Court recognized sexual harassment as a prohibited act under Title VII of the Civil Rights Act of 1964. "Without question, when a supervisor sexually harasses a subordinate because of a subordinate's sex, that supervisor discriminates on the basis of sex." In this case the Court found a legal violation even though the victim did not report the harassment nor utilize the existing grievance procedure. The court held that lack of knowledge of the harassment will not automatically shield the employer from liability.

Rabidue v. Oscela Refining Co., 805 F.2d 611 (6th Cir. 1986).
   The court ruled that Title VII was not designed to bring about a transformation in the social mores of American workers. The court held that maintaining a hostile or abusive working environment "must interfere with the job performance of a reasonable person in order for the behavior to be determined sexual harassment." This case is interesting because the "reasonable woman test" was first set out in Judge Drupansky's dissent.

Moire v. Temple University School of Medicine, 613 F. Supp. 1360 (E.D. Pa. 1985, aff'd 800 F. 2d 1136 (3d Cir. 1986).
   In this case the court stated that sexual harassment "demeans and degrades women." The court held that "abusive environment sexual harassment" was an actionable form of sexual harassment, and occurs where multiple incidents of offensive conduct lead to an environment violative of a victim's civil rights.

Scott v. Sears, Roebuck & Co., 605 F. Supp 1047, 37 FEP Cases 878 (N.D.Ill, 1986, affirmed 798 F.2d 210, 41 FEP 805 (7th Cir. 1986).
   Because coworkers do not have the power over a fellow employee to create a *quid pro quo* situation, the employer is liable for the actions of employees under EEOC guidelines "where the employer knows or should have known of the conduct, unless it can be shown that it took immediate and appropriate corrective action."

1987

Shaw v. Nebraska Department of Correctional Services, 666 F.Supp. 1330, (1987).
Male members of the promotion selection committee created a "sexist" environment by referring to the females as "girls," "honey," and "dear." In its holding the court implied that the correctional facility was required to eliminate the "sexist" environment.

1988

Lipsett v. University of Puerto Rico, 864 F.2d 881 (1st Cir. 1988).
This decision affirmed the definition in Rabidue of what constitutes a hostile or abusive working environment. However, "unless the fact finder keeps both the man's and the woman's perspective in mind the courts may be too ready to accept the offender's behavior as reasonable." This case also found that Title IX of the 1972 Education Amendments covers sexual harassment in a similar manner to Title VII's coverage. The court held that Title IX prohibits sexual harassment when it affects "tangible aspects" of employment or education, or is so "severe and pervasive" that it alters the work or education environment.

Lewellyn v. Celanese Corp, 693 (W.D.N.Y. 1988).
In this case a female truck driver received frequent threats and sexual solicitations from her coworkers. The coworkers had established a "club" to see which one would have sex with her. She complained to management, got nowhere, and eventually quit to seek medical attention after a male coworker exposed himself to her in the rest room. A federal court said that she had been "constructively discharged" and it is the same as an illegal firing.

Broderick v. Ruder, 46 FEP Cases 1272 (D.D.C. 1988).
A female employee was forced to work in an environment in which managers harassed her, and other female employees, by bestowing preferential treatment upon those who submitted to their sexual advances. The court ruled that consensual sexual relations among employees in exchange for tangible employment benefits can create a sexually hostile working environment for other employees.

Bennett v. Corroon & Black Corp., 845 F. 2d 104, 46 EDP P. 37, 955, 46 FEP Cases 1329 (5th Cir. 1988).
A female employee alleged sexual harassment where she was depicted in cartoons in the men's rest room engaging in crude and deviant sexual activities. Although the Court of Appeals concluded that the conduct in question constituted sexual harassment, it concluded that, because the employer had immediately changed management upon learning of the allegation and had continued to pay the employee her salary until she found another job, she was not entitled to further relief.

Karen Smith v. Hennepin Technical Center, et. al. 1988 WL 53400 (D.Minn.).
In this case students continuously complained to administrators about incidents of sexual harassment. The Court held that Hennepin Technical Center administrators should have known of the harassment and should have acted to stop and correct the harassment.

1989

Price Waterhouse v. Hopkins, 57LS 1165 (U.S. Supreme Court, May 1, (1989).
In this Title VII sex discrimination case, the Court held that when an employee has shown an employer's unlawful motive was involved in an employment decision, the burden of proof shifts to the employer to prove by a preponderance of the evidence that it would have taken the same action without regard to the unlawful motive. The Court agreed that sex stereotyping, such as was practiced by the accounting firm, violated Title VII. The preponderance of evidence test means that an employer must show only that more evidence than not is on its side.

Stoneking v. Bradford Area School Dist., 882 F.2d 720 (3rd Cir. 1989).
In this case, a male band director coerced a female high school student into engaging in various sexual acts with him on school grounds by physical force and threats. The school district had ignored complaints from other students whom the band director had previously attacked. The court ruled that the principal and assistant principal were not entitled to qualified immunity from liability where they maintained a policy, practice or custom of failing

to take action on students' complaints of sexual misconduct by teachers, which created a "climate that facilitated sexual abuse of students by teachers in general."

Fisher v. Tacoma School Dist. No. 10, 53 Wash. App. 591, 769 P.2d 318 (1989).
A female assistant custodian of a high school filed suit against the chief custodian for sexual harassment which involved, among other incidents, leaving an anonymous note on the custodians' lunch table that stated, "Discrimination is hard to prove."

1990

King v. Board of Regents University of Wis., 898 F.2d 522 (7th Cir. 1990).
A female assistant professor filed suit against a male assistant dean who had subjected her to suggestive innuendos, suggestive leering, offensive sexual touching, forcible kissing, and insistence that he "have her" in front of others. The federal court of appeals held that sexual harassment of public employees may violate the Fourteenth Amendment's Equal Protection Clause.

1991

Ellison v. Brady, 924 F.2d 872 (9th Cir. 1991).
In this case, the court established the "reasonable woman" standard. The court stated that, "Many women share common concerns which men do not necessarily share. For example, because women are disproportionately victims of rape and sexual assault, women have a stronger incentive to be concerned with sexual behavior. Women who are victims of mild forms of sexual harassment may understandably worry whether a harasser's conduct is merely a prelude to violent sexual assault. Men, who are rarely victims of sexual assault, may view sexual conduct in a vacuum without a full appreciation of the social setting of the underlying threat of violence that a woman may perceive."

Robinson v. Jacksonville Shipyards, 760 F.Supp. 1486 (M.D.Fla. 1991).
In this case, the court ruled that nude pin-ups in the workplace is sexual harassment. Robinson testified that pornographic pictures were displayed at 40 sites in the Jacksonville Shipyards and she found them offensive. The Robinson court took the case one step further by establishing that the pornographic pictures had a direct affect on working conditions. Male coworkers

made suggestive remarks to her when they were in the presence of the pornographic pictures. When she objected to the pictures, the sexual taunting increased, thus creating a hostile and intimidating working environment. The court ruled that even though some female employees did not complain of the work environment or find some behaviors objectionable, the fact that a "reasonable woman" would find that the working environment was abusive was sufficient to cause the court to rule in favor of the plaintiff.

Monohon v. Sullivan Payne Co. (Iowa Dist. Ct., Polk Cty., No. 70-41225, Novak, J., 6/12/91).
A female vice-president who was forced to resign because of sexual harassment was awarded $6.3 million from a former employer.

1992

Franklin v. Gwinnett County, GA Public Schools , 117 L. Ed 2d 209 (1992).
In this the U. S. Supreme Court granted certiorari to review a Title IX claim brought by a high school student against a school district employee and the school district. The Court ruled that students who claim they were sexually harassed may seek monetary damages, in addition to other remedies, when they sue that school and/or school officials. In this case, a female high school student filed a suit against a school district for sexual harassment by her teacher. The teacher, at first, gave the student special attention. He later followed her at school. Finally, he excused her from class and had sexual intercourse with her on school grounds. School officials were aware of this situation. The teacher resigned and all matters against him were dropped. Prior to this case, Title IX was thought to provide only injunctive relief to stop discriminatory practices.

Jane Doe v. Taylor I.S.D. 975 F.2d 137 (5th Cir. 1992).
The 5th Circuit has recently held that a student has a constitutional right to be free from sexual molestation by a state employed school teacher and that the superintendent and principal have an affirmative duty to protect a student from such an intrusion.

Appendix D
Equal Opportunity Commission Offices

Alabama
Equal Employment Opportunity
Commission
Birmingham District Office
1900 Third Avenue, North, Suite 101
Birmingham, Alabama 35203
205-731-0082

Arizona
Equal Employment Opportunity
Commission
Phoenix District Office
4520 North Central Avenue
Suite 300
Phoenix, Arizona 85012-1848
602-640-5000

Arkansas
Equal Employment Opportunity
Commission
Little Rock Area Office
320 West Capitol Avenue, Suite 621
Little Rock, Arkansas 72201
501-324-5060

California
Equal Employment Opportunity
Commission
Fresno Local Office
1313 P Street, Suite 103
Fresno, California 93721
209-487-5793

Equal Employment Opportunity
Commission
880 Front Street
Room 45-21
San Diego, California 92188
619-557-6288

Equal Employment Opportunity
Commission

Los Angeles District Office
3660 Wilshire Boulevard, Fifth Floor
Los Angeles, California 90010
213-251-7278

Equal Employment Opportunity
Commission
Oakland Local Office
1333 Broadway, Room 430
Oakland, California 94612
415-273-7588

Equal Employment Opportunity
Commission
San Francisco District Office
901 Market Street, Suite 500
San Francisco, California 94103
415-744-6500

Equal Employment Opportunity
Commission
San Jose Local Office
96 North Third Street, Suite 200
San Jose, California 95112
408-291-7352

Colorado
Equal Employment Opportunity
Commission
Denver District Office
1845 Sherman Street, Second Floor
Denver, Colorado 80203
303-866-1300

Washington, D.C.
Equal Employment Opportunity
Commission
Washington Field Office
1400 L Street NW, Suite 200
Washington, D.C. 20005
202-275-7377

Florida
Equal Employment Opportunity
Commission
Miami District Office
1 Northeast First Street, Sixth Floor
Miami, Florida 33132
305-536-4491

Equal Employment Opportunity
Commission
Tampa Area Office
Timberlake Federal Building Annex
501 East Polk Street, Suite 1020
Tampa, Florida 33602
813-228-2310

Georgia
Equal Employment Opportunity
Commission
Atlanta District Office
75 Piedmont Avenue, NE, Suite 1100
Atlanta, Georgia 30335
404-331-6093

Hawaii
Equal Employment Opportunity
Commission
Honolulu Local Office
677 Ala Moana Blvd., Suite 404
Honolulu, Hawaii 96813
808-541-3120

Illinois
Equal Employment Opportunity
Commission
Chicago District Office
536 South Clark Street, Room 930
Chicago, Illinois 60605
312-353-2713

Indiana
Equal Employment Opportunity
Commission
Indianapolis District Office
46 East Ohio Street

Room 456
Indianapolis, Indiana 46204
317-226-7212

Kentucky
Equal Employment Opportunity
Commission
Louisville Area Office
600 Martin Luther King Jr. Place,
Room 268
Louisville, Kentucky 40202
502-582-6082

Louisiana
Equal Employment Opportunity
Commission
New Orleans District Office
701 Loyola Avenue, Suite 600
New Orleans, Louisiana 70113
504-589-2329

Maryland
Equal Employment Opportunity
Commission
Baltimore District Office
111 Market Place, Suite 4000
Baltimore, Maryland 21202
301-962-3932

Massachusetts
Equal Employment Opportunity
Commission
Boston Area Office
1 Congress Street, Room 1001
Boston, Massachusetts 02114
617-565-3200

Michigan
Equal Employment Opportunity
Commission
Detroit District Office
477 Michigan Avenue, Room 1540
Detroit, Michigan 48226
313-226-7636

Minnesota
Equal Employment Opportunity
Commission
Minneapolis Local Office
220 Second Street South, Room 108
Minneapolis, Minnesota 55401-2141
612-370-3330

Mississippi
Equal Employment Opportunity
Commission
Jackson Area Office
Cross Road Building Complex
207 West Amite Street
Jackson, Mississippi 39201
601-965-4537

Missouri
Equal Employment Opportunity
Commission
Kansas City Area Office
911 Walnut Street, Tenth Floor
Kansas City, Missouri 64106
816-426-5773

Equal Employment Opportunity
Commission
St. Louis District Office
625 N. Euclid Street, Fifth Floor
St. Louis, Missouri 63108
314-425-6585

New Jersey
Equal Employment Opportunity
Commission
Newark Area Office
60 Park Place, Room 301
Newark, New Jersey 07102
201-645-63383

New Mexico
Equal Employment Opportunity
Commission
Albuquerque Area Office
505 Marquette, NW, Suite 1105

Albuquerque, New Mexico 87102-2189
505-766-2061

New York
Equal Employment Opportunity
Commission
Buffalo Local Office
28 Church Street, Room 301
Buffalo, New York 14202
716-846-4441

Equal Employment Opportunity
Commission
New York District Office
90 Church Street, Room 1501
New York, New York 10007
212-264-7161

North Carolina
Equal Employment Opportunity
Commission
Charlotte District Office
5500 Central Avenue
Charlotte, North Carolina 28212
704-567-7100

Equal Employment Opportunity
Commission
Greensboro Local Office
324 West Market Street, Room 27
PO Box 3363
Greensboro, North Carolina 27401
919-333-5174

Equal Employment Opportunity
Commission
1309 Annapolis Drive
Raleigh, North Carolina 27608
919-856-44064

Ohio
Equal Employment Opportunity
Commission
Cincinnati Area Office

The Ameritrust Building
525 Vine Street, Suite 810
Cincinnati, Ohio 45202
513-684-2851

Equal Employment Opportunity
Commission
Cleveland District Office
1375 Euclid Avenue, Room 600
Cleveland, Ohio 44115
216-522-2001

Oklahoma
Equal Employment Opportunity
Commission
Oklahoma City Area Office
531 Couch Drive
Oklahoma City, Oklahoma 73102
405-231-4911

Pennsylvania
Equal Employment Opportunity
Commission
Philadelphia District Office
1421 Cherry Street, Tenth Floor
Philadelphia, Pennsylvania 19102
215-656-7020

Equal Employment Opportunity
Commission
Pittsburgh Area Office
1000 Liberty Avenue, Room 2038-A
Pittsburgh, Pennsylvania 15222
412-644-3444

South Carolina
Equal Employment Opportunity
Commission
Greenville Local Office
15 South Main Street, Suite 530
Greenville, South Carolina 29601
803-241-4400

Tennessee
Equal Employment Opportunity
Commission
Memphis District Office
1407 Union Avenue, Suite 621
Memphis, Tennessee 38104
901-722-2617

Equal Employment Opportunity
Commission
Nashville Area Office
50 Vantage Way, Suite 202
Nashville, Tennessee 37228
615-736-5820

Texas
Equal Employment Opportunity
Commission
Dallas District Office
8303 Elmbrook Drive
Dallas, Texas 75247
214-767-7015

Equal Employment Opportunity
Commission
El Paso Area Office
The Commons Building C
Suite 103
4171 N. Mesa Street
El Paso, Texas 79902
915-534-6550

Equal Employment Opportunity
Commission
Houston District Office
1919 Smith Street, Seventh Floor
Houston, Texas 77002
713-653-3320

Equal Employment Opportunity
Commission
San Antonio District Office
5410 Fredricksburg Road, Suite 200
San Antonio, Texas 78229

Virginia
Equal Employment Opportunity
Commission
Norfolk Area Office
252 Monticello Avenue, First Floor
Norfolk, Virginia 23510
804-441-3470

Equal Employment Opportunity
Commission
Richmond Area Office
3600 West Broad Street, Room 229
Richmond, Virginia 23230
804-771-2692

Wisconsin
Equal Employment Opportunity
Commission
Milwaukee District Office
310 West Wisconsin Avenue
Suite 800
Milwaukee, Wisconsin 53203
414-297-1111

U.S. Department of Education
OCR
Mary E. Switzer Bldg.
330 C. Street, SW
Washington, D.C. 20202
202-205-5413

Appendix E
Other Gender Equity Resources

American Association of University
Women
2401 Virginia Avenue, NW
Washington, D.C. 20037
202-785-7700

American Bar Association
Commission on Women in the
Profession
750 North Lake Shore Drive
Chicago, IL 60611
312-988-5668

American Civil Liberties Union
Women's Rights Project
132 West 43rd Street
New York, NY 10036
212-944-9800

Asian-American Legal Defense and
Education Fund
99 Hudson Street
New York, NY 10013
212-966-5932

Asian Immigrant Women Advocates
310 8th Street, Suite 301
Oakland, CA 94607
510-268-0192

Assault
Box 21378
Washington, DC 20009
202-483-7165

Association of American Colleges
1818 R Street, NW
Washington, D.C. 20009
202-387-1300

Business and Professional
Women/USA
2012 Massachusetts Avenue, NW
Washington, D.C. 20036
202-293-1100

Center for Women and Policy Studies
2000 P Street, NW, Suite 508
Washington, DC 20036
202-872-1770

Coalition of Labor Union Women
15 Union Square
New York, NY 10003
212-242-0700

Equal Rights Advocates
1663 Mission Street, Suite 500
San Francisco, CA 94103
415-621-0505

Federally Employed Women Legal and
Education Fund
1400 Eye Street, NW
Washington, D.C. 20005
202-462-5253

Fund for the Feminist Majority
1600 Wilson Boulevard, Suite 704
Arlington, VA 22209
703-522-2501

"Kindness"
9307 West 74 Street
Merriam, KS 66204
913-432-5158

Lawyer's Committee for Civil Rights
Under the Law
1400 Eye Street, NW, Suite 400
Washington, D.C. 20005
202-321-1212

Mexican American Legal Defense and
Education Fund
1430 K Street, NW
Washington D.C. 20005
202-628-4074

Ms. Foundation for Women
Ad Hoc Sexual Harassment Coalition
141 Fifth Avenue
New York, NY 10010
212-353-8580

NAACP Legal Defense and
Educational Fund, Inc.
99 Hudson Street
New York, NY 10013
212-219-1900

National Association of Commissions
for Women
c/o D.C. Commission for Women
N-354 Reeves Center
2000 14th Street, NW
Washington, D.C. 20009
202-628-5030

National Association for Public
Interest Law
215 Pennsylvania Avenue
Washington, D.C. 20003
202-546-9707

National Association for Women in
Education
1325 18th Street, NW, Suite 210
Washington, D.C. 20036
202-659-9330

National Association of Working
Women: 9 to 5
1224 Hudson Road
Cleveland, OH 44113
216-566-9308

National Center for the Prevention and
Control of Rape
National Institutes for Mental Health
5600 Fishers Lane
Rockville, MD 20852
301-443-3728

National Conference of State
Legislatures Women's Network
1607 250th Avenue
Corwith, IA 50430
515-583-2156

National Council for Research on
Women
The Sara Delano Roosevelt Memorial
House
47-49 East 65 Street
New York, NY 10021
212-570-5001

National Education Association
Human and Civil Rights
1201 Sixteenth Street N.W.
Washington, D.C. 20036
202-822-7700

National Employment Law Project
236 Massachusetts Avenue, NE
Washington, DC 20002
202-544-2185

NOW Legal Defense Fund
National Association of Women and
the Law
99 Hudson Street, 12th Floor
New York, NY 10013
212-925-6635

National Women's Law Center
1616 P. Street NW
Washington, DC 20036
202-328-5160
Office of Personnel Management
1900 E Street, NW

Washington, D.C. 20415
202-606-1212

Pacific Resource Development Group
4044 NE 58 the Street
Seattle, WA 98105

Quality Work Environments
P.O. Box 1946
Manhattan, KS 66502
913-532-5533

STOP Violence Coalition
9307 West 74 Street
Merriam, KS 66204
913-432-5158

Survival Skills Education and
Development
1640 Fairchild, Suite 4
Manhattan, KS 66502
(913)776-4902
FAX (913)537-017

Trial Lawyers for Public Justice
2000 P Street, NW, Suite 611
Washington, DC 20036
202-463-8600

United States Student Association
815 15th Street, NW, Suite 838
Washington, DC 20005
202-347-8772

Wider Opportunities for Women
1324 G Street, NW
Washington, DC 20005
202-638-3143

Women Employed Institutes
22 West Monroe, Suite 1400
Chicago, IL 60603
312-782-3902

Women Organized Against Sexual
Harassment
PO Box 4768
Berkeley, CA 94704
415-642-7310

Women Students' Sexual Harassment
Caucus
Department of Applied Psychology
Ontario Institute for Studies in
Education
252 Bloor Street West
Toronto, Ontario M5S 1V6

Women's Action for Good
Employment Standards
c/o Institute for Research on Women's
Health
1616 18th Street, NW, #109 B
Washington, DC 20009
202-483-8643

Women's Law Project
125 South 9th Street, Suite 401
Philadelphia, PA 19107
215-928-9801

Women's Legal Defense Fund
1875 Connecticut Avenue, NW
 Suite 710
Washington, DC 20009
202-986-2600

Appendix F
Kids' Bill of Rights:

1. Kids have the right to be who they are.
2. Kids have the right to loved.
3. Kids have the right to be cared for when they're sick and well.
4. Kids have the right to be safe and protected.
5. Kids have the right to defend themselves when someone hurts them, and to get a grown-up to help.
6. Kids have the right to want and get attention and affection.
7. Kids have the right to be respected.
8. Kids have the right to make mistakes.
9. Kids have the right to get guidance from others.
10. Kids have the right to learn from others.
11. Kids have the right to ask questions.
12. Kids have the right to have feelings.
13. Kids have the right to say yes and no.
14. Kids have the right to choose what they like and don't like.
15. Kids have the right to agree and disagree with other kids and grown-ups.
16. Kids have the right to be with others sometimes.
17. Kids have the right to be alone sometimes.
18. Kids have the right to be different and unique.
19. No one has the right to physically hurt you--not grown-ups, not other kids.
20. No one has the right to sexually hurt you--not grown-ups, not other kids.

Reproduced by permission from Project Charlie, 4570 West 77th Street, Suite 198, Edina, MN 55435, 612-830-1432

Glossary of Terms

Although there are various definitions of each of the following terms, for the purpose of our discussion we will use the following:

Alienation
A state of estrangement from oneself, or society. Feminists argue that women's oppression in the home, in culture and in sexuality, creates a gender-specific form of women's alienation. And to the extent that men and women conform to stereotypes of masculinity and femininity, they will be alienated from each other in incompatible ways.

Androgyny
The psychological and psychic mixture of traditional masculine and feminine virtues comes from the Greek words andro (male) and gyn (female.) Many people believe that androgynous personalities are holistic and have a capacity to experience the full range of human emotions.

Constructive Notice
The employer under the conditions which existed should have known that sexual harassment was taking place; an implied notice.

Curriculum Theory
Although curriculum is usually thought of as a group of subjects based on disciplines operating a syllabus of material and a particular method of teaching. The overt and "hidden" curriculum are the conscious and unconscious ideology of any institution. Often the curriculum reinforces sex-role stereotyping by operating on a principle of "male as norm."

Equality
No individual should be less equal than any other. Judgements should be based upon individual merit rather than racial, ethnic, religious, social status, or gender.

Feminism
Feminism is an ideology of social transformation aimed at creating a world where women are liberated from all injustice because of their sex.

Hidden Curriculum

Education often includes material and messages that are not consciously planned. Often these messages reinforce sexual stereotyping. The hidden curriculum can include sex segregation in activities and programs or attitudes toward women exhibited by teachers and administrators.

Hostile Educational Environment

Unwelcome sexual conduct that unreasonably interferes with an individual's school performance or creates an intimidating, hostile or offensive environment.

Gender

We distinguish between sex and gender. Sex is biological and gender is behavioral. You are born to a sex, however, many of the traits often associated with being male or female are actually created by social pressures and conditioning.

Non-Verbal Harassment

Displaying of material that is sexually suggestive such as pornographic photos, jokes, or drawings. It can also be following a person, leering at a person's body, writing unwanted letters, or giving unwanted gifts.

Physical Harassment

Touching yourself or another person in a suggestive sexual manner.

Priming

Specific stimuli in the school environment prime certain categories for the application of stereotypical thinking (i.e. availability of photographs of nude and partially nude women, sexual joking, and sexual slurs, etc.).

Quid Pro Quo

Submission to or rejection of sexual conduct by an individual is used as the basis for educational decisions affecting the individual (something for something).

Respondeat Superior Liability

The employer is held liable where the person responsible for the sexual harassment is a supervisor.

Sex Bias

Sex bias is the character of behavior and attitudes resulting from belief in sex stereotypes and/or adherence to restrictively defined sex roles. The stereotype that women are not active, not independent, not competent, not able to take care of themselves, and are in need of help and protection is widespread and finds expression in our school classrooms.

Sexism

Any social relationship where a person or group is denigrated because of their sex. Sexism limits the activities and opportunities of its victims. Sexual stereotyping is an example of sexism.

Sex-Role Identity

Among the major determinants of sex-role identification of a young child are perceptions of similarity to others, and the adoption of behaviors traditionally encouraged for his or her sex. Sex-role identity is the degree to which an individual self-identifies with what is generally believed or accepted to be appropriate as masculine or feminine roles.

Sexual or Sex-based Behavior

Some kind of sexual connotation to the behavior or the behavior occurs because of the person's sex.

Sexual Favoritism

A student receives opportunities or benefits as a result of submission to a teacher's sexual advances.

Sexual Harassment

Unwelcome sexual advances, requests for sexual favors, and other verbal or physical conduct of a sexual nature.

Sex-Role

In our society, a role is the behavior expected of the occupant of a given position or status. Sex-role is then the behavior expected of men or women on the basis of biological sex.

Sex-Role Stereotype

Sex-role stereotypes are standardized, oversimplified conceptions of the behaviors that are appropriate to females and males. Sex-role stereotyping consists of forming expectations for the behavior of individual females and males on the basis of these stereotypes. In the stereotyping of sex roles, the qualities of the individual are ignored. It is difficult to contradict the social expectations that lead to this devaluing of the individual, often because of the belief that stereotyped traits are inborn, natural.

Sex Typing

Sex-typed characteristics are those characteristics associated with males and females. The three classes of sex-typed characteristics are (1) physical attributes (i.e. boys should be strong and large and that girls are petite and pretty), (2) overt behavior (i.e. boys are loud, aggressive and outgoing and girls are quiet, passive and shy), and (3) feelings, attitudes, motives, and beliefs (i.e. boys don't cry or have the ability to nurture and girls are naturally nurturing and emotional.)

Stereotyping

Stereotyping refers to a tendency for a belief to be widespread in any social group or society (e.g., "Women are emotional, Men are analytical"). According to Mitchell, it also denotes an oversimplification of a belief in regard to its content together with a tendency for the belief to be resistant to factual evidence to the contrary. People believe that their concepts of any particular group (e.g., women, men, blacks, oriental, whites, etc.) are accurate representations of real individuals in the group, whereas their conception is actually a stereotype acquired in some way other than direct experience. Because people mainly see what they expect to see, the situation is usually not improved even by direct experience. Stereotyped concepts are usually:

1. Simple rather than complex or differentiated.
2. Erroneous rather than accurate.
3. Acquired second hand rather than through direct experience with the reality it is supposed to represent.
4. Resistant to modification by new experience.

Unwelcome Sexual Advances

Even though the employee or student submits to sexual advances, the criteria to determine whether sexual harassment occurred is whether the sexual advancement was unwelcome.

Verbal Harassment

Telling sexual jokes or stories, making sexual comments about a person's body, sexual propositions, sexually suggestive, or obscene comments.

References

Allport, G., (1954). *The Nature of Prejudice*, Garden City New York: Doubleday Anchor Books.

Andelin, H., (1992). *Facinating Womanhood*, New York: Bantam Books.

Beauvais, K. (1986). *Workshops to Combat Sexual Harassment: a Case Study of Changing Atituedes.* Signs: A Journal of Women in Culture and Society, *121.*

Benson, A., (1984). *Comment of Crocker's "An Analysis of Univesity Definitions of Sexual Harsassment."* Signs: Journal of Women in culture and Society, *9.*

Bernard, C., and Schlaffer, E, (1983). *The Man in the Street: Why He Harasses, in Feminist Frontiers, (eds.)* Richardson, L, and Taylor, V, Reading, Massachusetts: Addison-Wesley.

Bryant, A.,(1993). *The Year of the Woman Gives Hope to Our Nation's Schoolgirls Gender Equity in Education Act Unveiled,* news release, Washington, D.C.: American Association of University Women (April 21).

Cadoff, J., (1993). *How To Raise A Strong Daughter In A Man's World,* Twins, January/February.

Center For Population Options. (1992). *Lesbian, Gay and Bisexual Youth: At Risk and Underserved,* Washingtion, D.C.: Center for Population Options.

Charren, P., (no date). Quoted in Cadoff, J., (1993). *How To Raise A Strong Daughter In A Man's World,Twins,*January.

Chodorow, N., (1971). *Being and Doing: A Cross Cultural Examination of Socialization of Males and Females,* in Gornick, V. and Moran, B. (eds.), Woman in Sexist Society, New York: Basic Books.

Chodorow, N., (1974). *Family Structure and Feminine Personality,* in Rosalado, M., and Lamphere, L. (eds.), Woman, Culture and Society. Stanford: Stanford University Press.

Coder-Mikinski, T., (1993). *Counselor Self-Efficacy and Suicide Intervention,* Unpublished Dissertation, University of Kansas.

Coopersmith, S., (1967). *Human Nature and the Social Order.* New York: Scribner.

David, D., and Brannon, R, (1976). *The Forty-nine Percent Majority: the Male Sex Role ,* New York: Random House.

EEOC Guidance Memorandum 6 to Field Personnel, 57, L.W. 2261 (Oct. 17, 1988)

Eskenazi, M. and Gallen, D., (1992). *Sexual Harassment: Know Your Rights!,* New York, Carroll & Graf Publishers, Inc.

Faludi, S., (1991), *Backlash: The Undeclared War Against American Women*, Crown Publishers, New York, N.Y.

Farley, L., (1978). *Sexual Shakedown*, New York, NY: Warner Books.

Fine, J., (1987, August 24-30). *No Laughing Matter: Sexual Harassment is Serious Problem for Companies. Dallas Times Herald*, pp; 9-11.

First, P., (1992). *Educational Policy for School Administrators*, Boston: Allyn & Bacon.

Fiske, S., (1991). Testimony appearing as an expert witness on plaintiff's behalf in the case *Robinson v. Jacksonville Shipyards, Inc.* 760 F.Supp. 1486 (M.D.Fla. 1991) at 1502.

French, M., (1992). *The War Against Women*, New York: Ballantine Books.

Fried, S., (1993). Conversations with authors April and May.

Gibson, P, (1989). *Gay Male and Lesbian Youth Suicide, Report of the Secretary's Task Force on Youth Sucide*, Washington, D.C.: U.S. Department of Health and Human Services.

Gilligan, C., (1982). *In a Different Voice: Psychological Theory and Women's Development.*, Cambridge, MA: Harvard Univerity Press.

Gleick, E., (1992). *The Boys On The Bus, People* Nov. 30, at 125.

Goldstein, L., (1992). *Feminist Jurisprudence*, Lanham, Maryland: Rowman & Littlefield Publishers, Inc.

Grauerholz, E., (1989). *Sexual Harassment of Women Professors by Students: Exploring the Dynamics of Power, Authority, and Gender in a University Setting.* Sex Roles, 21.

Hall, R., and Sandler, B., (no date). *The Classroom Climate: A Chilly One For Women?* Paper published by the Project of the Status and Education of Women, Washington D.C.: Association of American Colleges.

Hamachek, D., (1978). *Encounters With The Self* (2nd ed.) New York: Holt, Rinehart and Winston.

Harding, J., (1968). *Stereotypes.* In O. Sills (Ed.) *International encyclopedia of the social sciences*, 15. New York: Crowell, Collier and MacMilian, Inc.

Hess, R., (1992). *Sexual Assault Cover-up in Public Schools.* FACT: Friends of Alachua County Talk, (May).

Hostile Hallways: The AAUW Survey on Sexual Harassment in America's Schools, (1993). Washington, D.C.: American Association of University Women Educational Foundation.

Hostile Hallways: The AAUW Survey on Sexual Harassment in America's Schools, (1993). (Fact Sheet) Washington, D.C.: American Association of University Women Educational Foundation.

Hubbard-Harris, V., (1993). Conversation with the authors.

Hunter, J. and Schaecher, R. (1987). *Stresses on Lesbian and Gay Adolescents in Schools*, Social Work in Educaiton

Johnson, C, Stockdale, M, Saal, F, (1991). *Persistence of Men's Misperceptions of Friendly Cues Across a Variety of Interpersonal Encounters,* Psychology of Women Quarterly, 15 (1991) at 464.

Johnson, K. and Workman, J, (1992), *Clothing and Attributions Concerning Sexual Harasment, Home Economics Research Journal,* Vol. 21, No. 2, December, p. 161.

Jordan, J., (1986). *The Meaning of Mutuality,* Work In Progress # 23, Wellesley, MA: The Stone Center, Wellesley College.

Kagan, J., (1964). *Acquisition of Sex Typing and Sex-Role Idenity.* In Hoffmen, M & Hoffmen, L., (Ed.) *Review of Child Development Research.* New York: Russsell Sage Foundation.

Kaplan, H., (1975). *Self-Attitudes and Deviant Behavior,* Pacific Palisades, CA: Goodyear Publishing.

Kenig, J., and Ryan, *Sex Differences in Levels of Tolerance and Attribution of Blame for Sexual Harassment on a University Campus,* Sex Roles, 15, at 535.

LeClair, L., (1991). *Sexual Harassment Between Peers Under Title VII and TItle IX Why Girls Just Can't Wait to be Working Women,* Vermont Law Review, Vol. 6:30.

Lever, J., (1978). *Sex differences in the Complexity of Children's Games,* American Sociological Review.

Lever, J., (1976). *Sex Differences in the Games Children Play,* Social Problems.

Lewis, J., Hastings, S., and Morgan, A.,(1993). *Sexual Harassment in Education, National Organizaiton on Legal Problems of Education,* Topeka, Kansas.

Mackinnon, C., (1979). *Sexual Harassment of Working Women: A Case of Sex Discriminination,* New Haven: Yale University Press.

Manning, A., *School Girls Sexually Harassed, USA Today,* Wednesday, March 24, 1993, p1A.

Masters, A., (1992). *The Evolution of the Legal Concept of Environmental Sexual Harassment of U.S. Higher Education Students By Faculty,* Unpublished Dissertation, University of Florida.

Mawdsley, R. and Hampton, Frederick, (June 18, 1992). *Sexual Misconduct by School Emplolyees Involving Students*, West's Education Law Reporter, St. Paul, MN: West Publishing.

McClelland, D., (1974). *Power: The Inner Experience*, New York: Irvington Press

Mead, M., (1968).*Sex and Temperament in Three Primitive Societies*, New York: Dell, first published in 1935.

Mead, M., (1978), *A Proposal: We Need Tabos On Sex at Work. Redbook* (April).

Mitchell, G. (1968). *A Dictionary of Sociology*. Chicago: Aldine Publishing Co.

Money, J. and Ehrhardt, A., (1972). *Man and Woman, Boy and Girl,* Baltimore:Johns Hopkins University Press

National Association of Secondary School Principals, (1992). *Sexual Misconduct by School Employees*, A Legal Memorandum, Reston, VA: NASSP>

National Education Association, Human & Civil Rights Action Sheet, (no date) *Teaching And Counseling Gay andd Lesbian Students*, Washington, D.C.: NEA

National Gay and Lesbian Task Force, (1982). *Gay Rights in the United States and Canada*, New York, N.Y.: National Gay and Lesbian Task Force.

Omilian, S., (1987). *Sexual Harassment in Employment*, Deerfield, Illinois: Callaghan.

O'Gorman Hughes, J. and Sandler, B., (1988). *Peer Harassment: Hassles for Women on Campus*, Washington, D.C.: Project on the Status and Education of Women, Association of American Colleges.

O'Gorman Hughes, J. and Sandler, B., (1992) *In Case of Sexual Harassment: A guide for Women Students*, Washington, D.C.: Center for Women Policy Studies.

Palin, P., (1993). Mr. Palin is the Human Resources Manager for the South Washington County Schools, Cottage Grove, Minnesota. Conversations and written communication with the authors during the period between April 1, 1993 to April 28, 1993.

Pauldi, M. and Barickman, R., (1991). *Academic and Workplace Sexual Harassment*, Albany: State University of New York Press.

Petrocelli, W. and Repa, B., (1992). *Sexual Harassment On The Job*, Berkely, Claifornia: Nolo Press.

Piaget , J., (1965). *The Moral Judgement Of The Child*, New York: The Free Press.

Preventing Sexual Harassment in Utah State Government, (1989). Department of Human Resource Management, State of Utah.

Rauch, C., Sandquist, L., Stokes, A., (1993). Conversations and communications with the authors regarding the program on eradicating sexual harassment that has been implemented at Goodrich Middle School, Lincoln, NE.

Rosenberg, M. (1965). *Conceiving The Self,* New York: Basic Books.

Rubin, L., (1992). *Sexual Harassment: Individual Differences In Reporting Behaviors,* Unpublished doctoral dissertation, University of Kansas.

Saal, F., Johnson, C., & Weber, N. *"Friendly or Sexy?" It May Depend On Whom You Ask."* Psychology of Women Quarterly, 13, at 263-276.

Salomone, R., (1986).*Equal Education Under Law,* New York, St. Martin's Press.

Sandroff, R., (1992). *Sexual Harassment: The Inside Story, Working Woman Magazine,* (June).

Schneider (1987). *Graduate Women, Sexual Harassment and University Policy,* Journal of Higher Education, Vol 58. 46-65.

School Safety & the Legal Commuity, (1985). Westlake Village, CA: National School Safety Center.

Sexual Harassment in the Federal Government: An Update, A Report of the U.S. Merit Systems Protection Board Office of Merit Systems Review and Studies, Washington, D.C., June, 1988.

Sexual Harassment in the Federal Workplace, (March, 1981). A Report of the U.S. Merit Systems Protection Board Office of Merit Systems Review and Studies, Washington, D.C.

Shoop, R., and Edwards, D, (1992). *"Training Manual"* that accompanies the video program Sexual Harassment: *What is It and Why Should I Care?,* Manhattan, KS: Quality Work Environments, Inc.

Shoop, R. and Hayhow, J, (1993), *Sexual Harassment In Our Schools: What Parents and Teachers Need To Know To Spot It and Stop It,* Allyn & Bacon, Needham, MA.

Shrauger, J. & Lund, A. (1975). *Self-Evaluation And Reactions To Evaluations From Others. Journal of Personality,* 43.

Silva, T., (1992). *Students Tell Board of Sexual Harassment,* Gainesville Sun, (May 6).

Stein, N., Marshall, N., and Trop, L., (1993). *Secrets In Public: Sexual Harassment In Our Schools.* A report on the results of a *Seventeen* magazine survey. Center for Research on Women, Wellesley College.

Stoller, R., (1964). A Contribution To The Study Of Gender Idenity, *International Journal of Psycho-Analysis* 45, 220-226.

Surry, J. and Bergman, S., (1992). *The Woman-Man Relationship: Impasses and Possibilities,* Work In Progress # 55, Wellesley, MA: The Stone Center, Wellesley College.

Tannen, D., (1990). *You Just Don't Understand,* New York: Ballantine Books.

The AAUW Report: *How Schools Shortchange Girls,* (1992). Washington, D.C.: American Association of University Women Educational Foundation

Thurston, L., (1993). Conversations with authors.

Till, F. J. (1980). *Sexual Harassment: A Report On The Sexual Harassment Of Students.* Report of the National Advisory Council on Women's Educational Programs. Washington D.C: U.S. Department of Education.

Unell, B., (1993). Conversations with authors during April and May.

Valente, W., (July 30, 1992). *Liability for Teacher's Sexual Misconduct With Students-Closing and Opening Vistas,* West's Education Law Reporter, St. Paul, MN: West Publishing.

Villaume, P. and Foley, R., (1993). *Teachers At Risk,* Bloomington, MN: Villaume and Foley.

Walsh, C., (1993). *Openly Addressing Sexual Harassment In Schools,* School Safety Update, Westlake Village, CA: National School Safety Center, (April).

Webb, S., (1992). *Preventing Sexual Harassment In A Small Business,* Small Business Forum, (Fall).

Webb, S., (1991). *Sexual Harassment: Investigator's Manual* Premiere Publishing, Ltd.

Webb, S., (1991). *Step Forward: Sexual Harassment In The Workplace,* Mastermedia.

Williams, R., and Williams, V., (1993). *Anger Kills,* New York: Times Books

About the Authors

Robert J. Shoop is a professor of Educational Law at Kansas State University. He is the author or co-author of seven books, over 100 journal articles, and several monographs and book chapters on various legal issues. His most recent books are, *School Law for the Principal: A Handbook for Practitioners, A Primer for School Risk Management,* and *Sexual Harassment in Our Schools: What Parents and Teachers Need to Know to Spot It and Stop It,* all published by Allyn and Bacon.

He is the Co-founder and President of Quality Work Environments, Incorporated, a production and consulting company that has recently produced *Sexual Harassment: What Is It and Why Should I Care?* a video program on eliminating sexual harassment in the public schools. He is much sought as a speaker at national conferences and is a recognized authority in the area of legal issues in education and sexual harassment.

Dr. Shoop is a recipient of the Kansas State University Outstanding Teacher Award and is a member of the Board of Directors of the National Organization on Legal Problems of Education.

Debra L. Edwards is a elementary school principal in the Pottawatomie West School District, St. George, Kansas. She is Co-founder and Vice-President of Quality Work Environments, Incorporated and has consulted and presented workshops on school law and sexual harassment. Ms. Edwards has served on many State and National boards and is currently a member of the Kansas ACLU Board of Directors.

Also Available

Sexual Harassment: What Is It and Why Should I Care?, a video program on eradicating sexual harassment from schools.

To order, to receive a catalogue, or to receive information about consulting, write:

Quality Work Environments, Inc.
P.O. Box 1945
Manhattan, KS 66502

913-381-5333